THE ODYSSEY

Homer

AUTHORED by Fiona Zublin
UPDATED AND REVISED by Michelle Rosenberg

COVER DESIGN by Table XI Partners LLC
COVER PHOTO by Olivia Verma and © 2005 GradeSaver, LLC

BOOK DESIGN by Table XI Partners LLC

Published by GradeSaver LLC, www.gradesaver.com

First published in the United States of America by GradeSaver LLC. 2014

ISBN 978-1-60259-418-0

Printed in the United States of America

For other products and additional information please visit http://www.gradesaver.com

Day 3 - Discussion of Thought Questions

1. Agamemnon warns Odysseus not to trust women. Why do you think this is?

   Time: 5 minutes

   Discussion: Agamemnon was killed by the schemings of his wife, and he seems to lay most of the blame on her even though he was killed by her lover. Agamemnon also mourns the death of his lover Cassandra, but doesn't acknowledge that she is a woman too and thus apparently untrustworthy. It seems that, to Agamemnon, Clytemnestra's greatest sin might be her betrayal.

2. Alcinous decides that all his nobles must give treasure to Odysseus and says they should tax their subjects to pay for it. Do you think this is a fair way to govern?

   Time: 5 minutes

   Discussion: Alcinous does mention that his nobles are always in his house eating his food, and thus he may have a host's prerogative to ask them for a favor in return. This is not the same as a social contract between a government and its citizens, however. Also, the peasants don't know Odysseus or share in any of the spoils of Alcinous' hall.

3. The Phaeacians see their ship wrecked, presumably by Poseidon, and their first response is not to rail against the god but to sacrifice many bulls to him. What does this say about the relation of the ancient Greeks to their gods?

   Time: 5 minutes

   Discussion: The gods of Olympus are capricious and violent, but it seems the Phaeacians have decided that there is no way to fight them and so appeasement is the only option. Also, religion is such a pervasive part of their culture that this kind of behavior on the part of the gods is accepted and normalized.

4. Why do you think the swineherd loved Odysseus so much?

   Time: 5 minutes

   Discussion: The tone of the Odyssey is very nostalgic--this is a legend of heroes and gods--and the swineherd's longing for the past and inability to see its flaws reflects that of the story's narrator, who is constantly heaping praise on Odysseus and the story's other protagonists. It also simply builds up Odysseus as a good and righteous person and ruler.

5. Why do you think the story of Agamemnon's murder is repeated so many times in the *Odyssey*?

   Time: 5 minutes

   Discussion: The story of Agamemnon provides a contrast to that of Odysseus. While Clytemnestra took up with another man and conspired to plot her husband's murder, Penelope has patiently waited for her husband all these years. It could also serve to heighten the tension, either for us or for Odysseus, seeing examples of other faithless women and worrying that Penelope will follow suit.

Day 3 - Short Answer Quiz

1. What does Elpenor ask be planted on his grave?

____

2. What do the ghosts need in order to recognize and talk to humans?

____

3. Why did Ajax's ghost refuse to speak to Odysseus?

____

4. Who is Sisyphus?

____

5. What does Circe tell Odysseus to do when he meets the Sirens?

____

6. Why did Eurylochus encourage the sailors to eat the Cattle of the Sun?

____

7. What does Athena disguise herself as when she appear to Odysseus in Ithaca?

____

8. Why does Athena go to Sparta?

____

9. Who does Odysseus visit first in Ithaca?

____

10. What does the swineherd lend Odysseus before they go to sleep?

____

Short Answer Quiz Key

1. An oar
2. To drink sacrificial blood.
3. Ajax was still angry that Odysseus had gotten the armor of Achilles when Ajax wanted it.
4. A man sentenced to push a rock up a hill for eternity in Hades, only to have it fall back down every time.
5. Stuff his men's ears with wax and tie himself to the mast so he can't follow them.
6. So they wouldn't die of starvation.
7. A shepherd boy.
8. To get Telemachus to return.
9. The swineherd who is still loyal to him.
10. A spare cloak.

Day 3 - Crossword Puzzle

ACROSS

2. Odysseus battles ____ and Charybdisla
7. Odysseus is constantly referred to as a "man of ____ and turns."
8. In what state do the Phaeacians leave Odysseus on Ithaca?
9. A light spear
11. Where does Athena go to fetch Telemachus?
13. Who is the Greek god of death?
16. What do Odysseus' men stuff in their ears to resist the Sirens?
17. Tantalus is forever reaching for and never able to grasp what?
18. Odysseus is warned that his men must not eat the Cattle of the ____
19. The central spar of a ship
20. First ghost to appear to Odysseus in the Underworld

DOWN

1. Whose song lures men to their deaths?
3. Agamemnon brings her from Troy back to Greece
4. A person on the run from retaliation for past crimes
5. Die of hunger
6. One who can predict the future
10. Days Odysseus drifts before reaching Calypso's island
12. Which Greek hero refuses to speak to Odysseus in the Underworld?
14. Which animal does Eumaeus keep?
15. The steering apparatus of a ship

Crossword Puzzle Answer Key

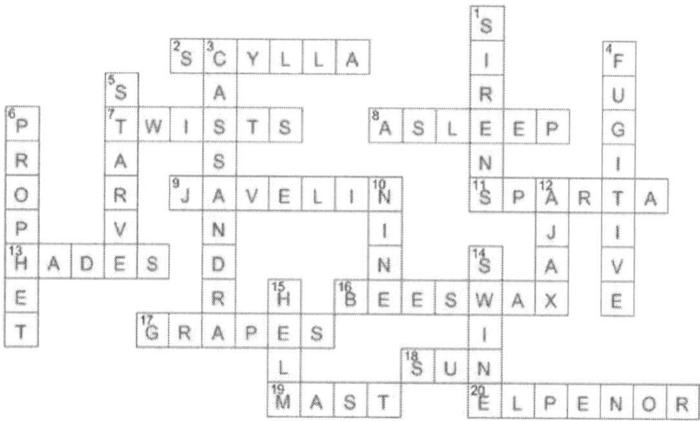

ACROSS

2. Odysseus battles _____ and Charybdisla
7. Odysseus is constantly referred to as a "man of _____ and turns."
8. In what state do the Phaeacians leave Odysseus on Ithaca?
9. A light spear
11. Where does Athena go to fetch Telemachus?
13. Who is the Greek god of death?
16. What do Odysseus' men stuff in their ears to resist the Sirens?
17. Tantalus is forever reaching for and never able to grasp what?
18. Odysseus is warned that his men must not eat the Cattle of the _____
19. The central spar of a ship
20. First ghost to appear to Odysseus in the Underworld

DOWN

1. Whose song lures men to their deaths?
3. Agamemnon brings her from Troy back to Greece
4. A person on the run from retaliation for past crimes
5. Die of hunger
6. One who can predict the future
10. Days Odysseus drifts before reaching Calypso's island
12. Which Greek hero refuses to speak to Odysseus in the Underworld?
14. Which animal does Eumaeus keep?
15. The steering apparatus of a ship

Day 3 - Vocabulary Quiz

Terms

1. ____ pyre
2. ____ shambling
3. ____ flitter
4. ____ magnanimous
5. ____ ebb
6. ____ grisly
7. ____ scourge
8. ____ strait
9. ____ blunder
10. ____ keel
11. ____ stockade
12. ____ paltry

Answers

A. a mound of flammable material, often used for burning dead bodies in a funeral rite
B. the timber underlying the structure of a ship
C. a fence made of stakes
D. to move quickly but without purpose
E. generous, kind
F. wander clumsily
G. horrible, disgusting
H. a menace
I. channel of water connecting two large bodies of water or seas
J. decline, diminish
K. scant, insufficient
L. shuffling, with a halting gait

Vocabulary Quiz Answer Key

1. A
2. L
3. D
4. E
5. J
6. G
7. H
8. I
9. F
10. B
11. C
12. K

Day 3 - Classroom Activities

1. Holding Out for a Hero

Kind of Activity: Classwide Discussion
Objective: To formulate complex ideas about virtue and lack thereof, and how the virtues we value shape our culture
Common Core State Standards: CCSS.ELA-Literacy.CCRA.R.6 ; CCSS.ELA-Literacy.CCRA.R.3
Time: 30 minutes

Structure:

Have a classwide discussion about what makes somebody a hero. Determine which characters in the *Odyssey* fit this definition. Is Odysseus actually the hero of his own story? Or is he simply the protagonist? Students should be able to talk about the character of Odysseus and what kind of culture would value his particular skills and virtues.

As a group, students should come up with lists of qualities that heroes possess and qualities they generally lack. Students should then analyze the characters of the story and discuss who they think is really the hero of the *Odyssey*. Also introduce the concept of the tragic hero in the classical sense. Talk about how Odysseus does and does not fit that mold.

Ideans for Differentiated Instruction:

-The class could divide into small groups and have separate discussions, then present their findings and opinions to the larger class.

-Students could present visual or video representations of depictions of heroes in other stories to support their ideas about what a hero does and is.

Assessment Ideas:

-During the class discussion, assess students' ability to synthesize complex ideas about morality and to marshall evidence from the text to support their opinions and ideas.

-Have students write short assessments based on their takeaway from the discussion and assess those written pieces.

2. Epic vs. Epic

Kind of Activity: Research
Objective: Students should understand the place of The Odyssey in the canon of Western literature
Common Core State Standards: CCSS.ELA-Literacy.CCRA.SL.2 ; CCSS.ELA-Literacy.CCRA.R.9
Time: 30 minutes

Structure:

Divide students into small groups. Each group should research and give a short presentation on other ancient epics and compare the hero to Odysseus. Good examples would be the *Aeneid*, *Beowulf*, or the Epic of Gilgamesh. You can assign each group its own ancient epic or task them with finding their own.

Next, as a group, students should discuss the individual presentations in the context of the journey narrative so common to these stories. What kinds of journeys do these other heroes go on and what does that say about the culture that produced them? How are they different from the *Odyssey* and how are they similar? Again, compare the classical Aristotelian concept of the hero to those of other cultures.

Ideans for Differentiated Instruction:

-Each student could choose to focus on a separate aspect of their epic — say, the role of women, the presence of monsters, the mode by which the hero travels, etc.

-Students could bring in additional elements by making short video presentations or in-class skits where they play different characters from other ancient epics.

Assessment Ideas:

-Based on the class discussion, assess the students' understanding of how ancient Greek culture shaped the values of the *Odyssey*, and their ability to apply that to other texts.

-Students should turn in their notes and presentations for evaluation.

Day 4 - Reading Assignment

Books 15-20

Common Core Objectives

- CCSS.ELA-Literacy.CCRA.R.5 Analyze the structure of texts, including how specific sentences, paragraphs, and larger portions of the text (e.g., a section, chapter, scene, or stanza) relate to each other and the whole.
- CCSS.ELA-Literacy.CCRA.W.3 Write narratives to develop real or imagined experiences or events using effective technique, well-chosen details and well-structured event sequences.
- CCSS.ELA-Literacy.CCRA.W.5 Develop and strengthen writing as needed by planning, revising, editing, rewriting, or trying a new approach.

Note that it is perfectly fine to expand any day's work into two days depending on the characteristics of the class, particularly if the class will engage in all of the suggested classroom exercises and activities and discuss all of the thought questions.

Content Summary for Teachers

Book 15: Athena visits Telemachus, still in Sparta, in a dream. She plays on his fear that his mother will get married and urges him to return home. Athena also warns Telemachus that some of Penelope's suitors are lying in wait to kill him and suggests an alternate route home. She tells him to stay his first night home with the loyal swineherd. When Telemachus wakes up, he sets out for home despite Menelaus' protestations. Along the way he picks up Theoclymenus, a seer who is fleeing his own land. Meanwhile, in Ithaca, Odysseus asks the swineherd for directions to the king's palace, but the swineherd warns him away from the suitors. The swineherd then tells him that Odysseus' father is still alive but his mother has died, and details his own life as a slave after he was betrayed by a Phoenician servant and taken from his home island. He then predicts that Telemachus and his line will reign in Ithaca forever. They land, and Telemachus sets off for the house of the loyal swineherd.

Book 16: Telemachus arrives at the swineherd's hut. Odysseus, still in disguise, encourages Telemachus to fight back against the suitors and throw them out. Telemachus dispatches the swineherd to tell Penelope he's home, but cautions him not to tell anyone else--not even Odysseus' father, Laertes, who has stopped eating since Telemachus went away. Athena appears to Odysseus, makes him look younger and handsomer, and urges him to reveal his identity to his son. He does and they are very happy to see each other, but Telemachus is still concerned as to how the two of them will fight off Penelope's suitors. Odysseus says Athena will help them and sends Telemachus home. Odysseus plans to infiltrate the palace disguised as a beggar and signal Telemachus when it is time to begin fighting. A herald and the swineherd tell Penelope that Telemachus is back, and several of her suitors plot to kill him. Penelope's servants overhear the plans and inform her; she berates the suitors for their treachery until one of them calms her down and she goes to sleep.

Book 17: Telemachus returns to the swineherd's hut and tells him to send the disguised Odysseus into town to beg. Telemachus himself goes back to the palace with some of his shipmates, and tells Penelope that Odysseus is captive on Calypso's island. The seer Theoclymenus assures her that Odysseus must be back in Ithaca, according to the signs. On the way into the city, the goatherd Melanthius passes them and taunts Odysseus for being a beggar. Eumaeus calls down Zeus' curse on Melanthius and they continue on. Argos, Odysseus' old dog, sees them and senses Odysseus near, then dies. Odysseus begs from the suitors and Antinous is rude to him, despite rebuke from Telemachus. Antinous throws a stool at Odysseus, who curses him. Penelope calls in the beggar, hoping he'll have news of Odysseus from abroad. He agrees to come after sundown, ostensibly to avoid the suitors.

Book 18: Another beggar, Arnaeus, picks a fight with Odysseus. The suitors encourage them to brawl, with the prize being a fresh sausage and permission to eat with the suitors from now on. Odysseus wins the fight, and while eating with the suitors he warns Amphinomous that a reckoning is on its way. Athena inspires Penelope to appear before her suitors, but while her maids are assembling Penelope falls asleep and Athena makes her radiantly beautiful. Penelope chides Telemachus for letting the suitors host a fight in her home and demurs in the face of the suitors' compliments. She demands gifts from her suitors, and they each send a page back to their estates to bring her an expensive present. Meanwhile, Odysseus tells the housemaids to go sit with the Queen. Athena inspires a fight: one of the suitors, Eurymachus, gets into a squabble with Odysseus and Telemachus has to smooth it over.

Book 19: Under cover of night, Odysseus and Telemachus hide the suitors' weapons. Odysseus (still disguised as a beggar) approaches Penelope, and Melantho the maid is rude to him for a second time. He and Penelope both lash out at the maid, and Penelope asks the apparent beggar if he has heard anything about Odysseus in his travels. She explains how she's strung along her suitors for years and describes her pretense of weaving a shroud for Laertes, which took her three years before they caught her undoing all her work in the night. Odysseus-as-beggar claims to have met Odysseus, and is able to describe him so well that Penelope breaks down in tears. He tells her he is certain Odysseus will return. Eurycleia, Telemachus' nurse, washes Odysseus' feet and recognizes him from an old scar on his leg, but he makes her swear not to reveal his identity. She offers to report on which of the house's women are loyal to him and which are loyal to the suitors, and he tells her he can judge that himself. Penelope returns and tells him about her dream: an eagle swooped down and killed her pet geese, and the eagle told her he was her husband and the geese were her suitors. Penelope decides to set the suitors a test: They must fire an arrow straight through twelve axes.

Book 20: Odysseus is visited in his sleep by Athena, who gives him a pep talk, while Penelope prays for death. Odysseus wakes to hear her and prays to Zeus for a good omen. He hears a maid in the hall asking Zeus that this be the last day she sees the suitors, and takes that as a good sign. The suitors arrive, and Telemachus sits Odysseus (still dressed as a beggar) down to eat with them. One of the suitors, Ctesippus, throws a cow's hoof at Odysseus, and Telemachus threatens to kill the suitor. Athena inspires crazed laughter in the suitors, and the room turns into a weird, ghastly vision where the walls run with blood—but the suitors don't notice. The seer Theoclymenus sees it for what it is: a very, very bad omen.

Thought Questions (students consider while they read)

1. Amphinomus shows kindness toward Odysseus, but that doesn't affect his fate. Is this fair or just?
2. Odysseus is often represented in dreams and omens as an eagle. Why do you think that is?
3. Do you think it's fair to punish the suitors for behavior that Athena inspired in them?
4. In this section, while dressed as a beggar, Odysseus often throws insults at those who are his social inferiors—the beggar Irus, for example, or the maid Melantho. Does this seem like heroic behavior to you?
5. Odysseus has several affairs while on the way home from Troy, while the idea of Penelope even considering remarriage is thought to be dishonorable. Do you think this is fair? What does it say about the values of the ancient Greeks?

Vocabulary (in order of appearance)

Book 15:

- cauldron: large metal pot
- colonnade: a row of columns supporting a roof
- libation: a drink poured out to honor a god
- fugitive: a person running away from consequences

Book 16:

- tally: score, sum

Book 18:

- javelin: a thin, light spear
- anguish: suffering, be it mental or physical
- pandemonium: chaos

Book 20:

- gallant: a man who flirts with women

Additional Homework

1. Seek out a few other translations of Homer's *Odyssey*, particularly Richmond Lattimore's. Choose a small block of text and compare and contrast the different translations. How do rhythm and rhyme scheme affect the way the story is told?
2. Watch the *Simpsons* episode entitled "Tales From the Public Domain" and analyze the part that retells the story of The Odyssey. What did they leave out? What did they get right?

Day 4 - Discussion of Thought Questions

1. Amphinomus shows kindness toward Odysseus, but that doesn't affect his fate. Is this fair or just?

   Time: 5 minutes

   Discussion: While it may not seem just for all the suitors, regardless of behavior, to die, it is typical of the Greek gods we've seen thus far. Students might contrast Poseidon's pitiless revenge on Odysseus with Athena's inability to forgive any of the suitors as the poem approaches its denouement.

2. Odysseus is often represented in dreams and omens as an eagle. Why do you think that is?

   Time: 5 minutes

   Discussion: Students may note that the eagle is a regal, military bird, and Odysseus is a nobleman, statesman, and military hero. Eagles are also seen as smart and ruthless, two traits and Odysseus is repeatedly praised for. Additionally, the eagle is associated with Zeus, who has been protecting Odysseus.

3. Do you think it's fair to punish the suitors for behavior that Athena inspired in them?

   Time: 10 minutes

   Discussion: Much of the behavior in this section of the book is directly pushed upon the characters by divine power. Students will probably conclude that the suitors are being punished for their self-initiated schemes to marry Penelope and kill Telemachus, rather than for their rudeness and violence inspired directly by a goddess. However, you could also use this as a jumping off point for questions about free will.

4. In this section, while dressed as a beggar, Odysseus often throws insults at those who are his social inferiors—the beggar Irus, for example, or the maid Melantho. Does this seem like heroic behavior to you?

   Time: 5 minutes

   Discussion: The characters in the *Odyssey* are sometimes painfully human—they don't do well at suffering in silence or staying polite when they are attacked. Thus far, students may conclude that Odysseus is within his rights to trade verbal barbs, though that may become less clear-cut with the violence of the book's denouement. Nevertheless, even Odysseus' less-than-noble behavior toward his inferiors is part of his heroism, in the Greek sense of heroes as larger-than-life figures with certain important talents, and other tragic flaws.

5. Odysseus has several affairs while on the way home from Troy, while the idea of Penelope even considering remarriage is thought to be dishonorable. Do you think this is fair? What does it say about the values of the ancient Greeks?

   Time: 5 minutes

   Discussion: Women in the *Odyssey* are defined entirely by their relations to men. Odysseus' honor is not damaged by his adultery because he exists independently of his relationships with women and his affairs don't seem to taint his other actions. His adultery does not even appear to considered sinful, which says a great deal about Greek attitudes toward male sexual infidelity.

Day 4 - Short Answer Quiz

1. With whom does Theoclymenus seek refuge?

___

2. Where does Telemachus first encounter Odysseus?

___

3. Who is Argo?

___

4. How does Odysseus disguise himself to fool Penelope's suitors?

___

5. What does Odysseus urge Telemachus to do when they finally reunite?

___

6. Who is Melanthius?

___

7. What dream does Penelope describe to the disguised Odysseus?

____

8. What did Laertes do when Telemachus left Ithaca?

____

9. How did Odysseus get the leg scar by which Eurycleia recognizes him?

____

10. What does Antinous throw at the beggar Odysseus?

____

Short Answer Quiz Key

1. With Telemachus on his ship bound for Ithaca.
2. In Eumaeus' hut, where both are staying.
3. Odysseus' dog, who senses his disguised master and then dies quietly.
4. He dresses as a beggar.
5. Challenge and defeat all his mother's suitors.
6. A goatherd who taunts Odysseus when he's dressed in beggar's garb.
7. An eagle swooping down and killing her pet geese.
8. He stopped eating.
9. He was hunting boars.
10. A stool.

Day 4 - Crossword Puzzle

ACROSS

3. What is Eurycleia's job in the palace?
5. A very large, formal dinner
9. Which birds represent the suitors in Penelope's dream?
11. The river in Egypt Odysseus claims to have visited
13. Which bird often represents Odysseus?
14. Which god owns the Cattle of the Sun?
15. A ritual drink poured out to honor a god
17. deadly
18. Telemachus "seals" Penelope's belief that Odysseus will return with a ___
19. The beggar who picks a fight with Odysseus
20. Which animal injured Odysseus and gave him a distinctive leg scar?

DOWN

1. Where did Odysseus, in disguise, claim to have met Odysseus?
2. Which maid is rude to Odysseus?
4. What species is Odysseus' pet Argos?
6. To which goddess does Penelope pray for death?
7. Who does Athena enchant to be radiantly beautiful?
8. A swindler or liar
10. An old hand, an experienced person, particularly a soldier
12. What does Antinous throw at the disguised Odysseus?
16. Who is Theoclymenus?

Crossword Puzzle Answer Key

															1 C		2 M
													3 N	U	R	S	E
															E		L
				4 D							5 F	E	6 A	S	T		A
				O				7 P					R		E		N
		8 C		9 G	E	E	S	E			10 V		T				T
		H						11 N	I	L	E		E				H
12 S		A		13 E	A	G	L	E			T		M				O
T		R						L		14 H	E	L	I	O	S		
O		15 L	I	B	A	T	I	O	N		R		S				
O		A						P			A				16 S		
17 L	E	T	H	A	L			E		18 S	N	E	E	Z	E		
		A													E		
19 A	R	N	A	E	U	S						20 B	O	A	R		

ACROSS

3. What is Eurycleia's job in the palace?
5. A very large, formal dinner
9. Which birds represent the suitors in Penelope's dream?
11. The river in Egypt Odysseus claims to have visited
13. Which bird often represents Odysseus?
14. Which god owns the Cattle of the Sun?
15. A ritual drink poured out to honor a god
17. deadly
18. Telemachus "seals" Penelope's belief that Odysseus will return with a ___
19. The beggar who picks a fight with Odysseus
20. Which animal injured Odysseus and gave him a distinctive leg scar?

DOWN

1. Where did Odysseus, in disguise, claim to have met Odysseus?
2. Which maid is rude to Odysseus?
4. What species is Odysseus' pet Argos?
6. To which goddess does Penelope pray for death?
7. Who does Athena enchant to be radiantly beautiful?
8. A swindler or liar
10. An old hand, an experienced person, particularly a soldier
12. What does Antinous throw at the disguised Odysseus?
16. Who is Theoclymenus?

Day 4 - Vocabulary Quiz

Terms	Answers
1. ____ cauldron	A. suffering, be it mental or physical
2. ____ colonnade	B. score, sum
3. ____ libation	C. chaos
4. ____ fugitive	D. a man who flirts with women
5. ____ tally	E. a drink poured out to honor a god
6. ____ javelin	F. large metal pot
7. ____ anguish	G. a thin, light spear
8. ____ pandemonium	H. a person running away from consequences
9. ____ gallant	I. a row of columns supporting a roof

Vocabulary Quiz Answer Key

1. F
2. I
3. E
4. H
5. B
6. G
7. A
8. C
9. D

Day 4 - Classroom Activities

1. Odyssey-Us

Kind of Activity: Creative Writing
Objective: To understand how nostalgia and point of view can affect a story.
Common Core State Standards: CCSS.ELA-Literacy.CCRA.W.3 ; CCSS.ELA-Literacy.CCRA.R.5
Time: 45 minutes

Structure:

Each student should write about his or her own odyssey--a journey he or she took or is currently on. Instruct them to write the story with themselves as hero, to embellish as needed and to skew every incident to make it clear that they themselves saved the day.

After they have had some time to write, have students present their stories to the class, and discuss what actually happened and how they embellished or changed the events to give the story the angle they wanted. Then, as a class, discuss what might have actually happened to Odysseus before he embellished the incidents of the *Odyssey*. Talk about the importance of storytelling, both in today's culture and in a culture that depended entirely on oral tradition for entertainment.

Ideans for Differentiated Instruction:

-Students could either submit their stories directly to the teacher or be asked to do a class presentation.

-Students could record audio stories or write their odysseys via blog posts or twitter messages.

Assessment Ideas:

-Have students turn in their stories (audio files, blog URLs, etc.) for evaluation by the instructor.

-Assess the students' engagement during the class discussion.

2. Poetic Justice

Kind of Activity: Creative Writing
Objective: To understand the bounds of poetic form while reforming the ideas of the Odyssey in their own words
Common Core State Standards: CCSS.ELA-Literacy.CCRA.W.5 ; CCSS.ELA-Literacy.CCRA.W.3
Time: 45 minutes

Structure:

As a group, lay out the events of the *Odyssey* in a simple timeline format. Then, break the students into groups and have each group choose an event to summarize using a simple poetic meter and rhyme scheme (for instance, ABABCC, a couple of stanzas). The class will end up with a poem that encompasses each major incident of Odysseus' journey from Troy to Ithaca. (A Google Doc or other shareable online word processing platform might be helpful here.)

The students should then analyze the work they've done, making sure that each verse not only lays out the events that took place in the story but the consequences the events had for Odysseus' journey. Talk about the episodic structure of the *Odyssey* and the way the author builds tension by delaying the inevitable climax of the story. What were the challenges of writing in verse? How does it make the story more effective than it would be if it were told in prose?

Ideans for Differentiated Instruction:

-If any students are musically inclined, they could write their section as a song.

-Students could work together in small groups or work as one very large group. Each group could perform the poems for each other.

Assessment Ideas:
-The poems should be handed in for assessment by the instructor.

Day 5 - Reading Assignment

Book 21-24

Common Core Objectives

- CCSS.ELA-Literacy.CCRA.R.7 Integrate and evaluate content presented in diverse media and formats, including visually and quantitatively, as well as in words.
- CCSS.ELA-Literacy.CCRA.R.1 Read closely to determine what the text says explicitly and to make logical inferences from it; cite specific textual evidence when writing or speaking to support conclusions drawn from the text.
- CCSS.ELA-Literacy.CCRA.W.9 Draw evidence from literary or informational texts to support analysis, reflection, and research.
- CCSS.ELA-Literacy.CCRA.R.2 Determine central ideas or themes of a text and analyze their development; summarize the key supporting details and ideas.

Note that it is perfectly fine to expand any day's work into two days depending on the characteristics of the class, particularly if the class will engage in all of the suggested classroom exercises and activities and discuss all of the thought questions.

Content Summary for Teachers

Book 21: Penelope fetches Odysseus' bow from storage—she tells the suitors that she will marry whoever can string the bow and shoot an arrow through twelve axes. Telemachus tries and fails to string the bow, as do each of the the suitors in turn. Meanwhile, Odysseus reveals his identity to Eumaeus and a loyal cowherd. Antinous suggests they try the bow again tomorrow after making sacrifices to Apollo, but Odysseus appears and asks if he can have a turn. Antinous berates and ridicules him, but Penelope and Telemachus argue for the disguised Odysseus, who easily strings the bow and shoots the arrow through the axes.

Book 22: With his next arrow, Odysseus shoots Antinous in the throat. Odysseus reveals his identity to the suitors, who try to blame their behavior on Antinous. When they see that won't work, they try to fight, but Odysseus and Telemachus kill all of them. The goatherd Melanthius crawls into the storeroom to retrieve the suitors' armor, and for that Eumaeus and the cowherd tie him to a cord and hoist him into the rafters. Athena appears, disguised as a man, and the suitors beg for help but she shouts encouragement to Odysseus and then perches in the rafters in the form of a bird. The suitors band together but are killed en masse. Telemachus asks for mercy for Phemius the bard and Medon the herald. Odysseus, covers in blood, asks Eurycleia which women in the house are loyal to him, and she tells him about a dozen women are not. Odysseus instructs Telemachus to make those women clean the hall of blood and then to kill them. Telemachus decides the sword is too honorable for these maids and hangs them instead. Melanthius is hauled into the hall and they cut off his hands, feet, nose, ears and genitalia, which are fed to dogs. Finally, Odysseus greets the rest of his loyal house, and they are all very happy to see him.

Book 23: Eurycleia wakes Penelope to tell her that Odysseus has returned and the suitors are dead. Penelope is suspicious, though, and worries it may be a trick of the gods. She greets Odysseus with ambivalence, and despite Telemachus' protestations, Odysseus accepts that she must test him. Odysseus, worried about the public backlash for his murdering of the suitors, tells Telemachus to prepare the house and make it seem as if there's a wedding feast going on, so nobody outside will be suspicious. Meanwhile, Penelope tests Odysseus by telling her maid to bring their wedding bed downstairs. Odysseus protests—he built the bed himself around a tree, and it cannot be moved. Penelope is overjoyed, and Odysseus tells her all about his travels and reveals that it is prophesied that he will have to go on another journey. The next day, Odysseus and Telemachus travel together to find Odysseus' father, Laertes.

Book 24:

In Hades, the ghosts of Agamemnon and Achilles argue over which of them had the better death. They encounter one of Penelope's suitors, Amphimedon, and find out how he was killed. Amphimedon primarily blames Penelope for the many deaths of the previous day.

Meanwhile, Odysseus visits his father, who doesn't recognize him. Initially, Odysseus pretends to be a stranger, but when he sees how he has upset his father, he reveals his true identity. Elsewhere, Ithaca discovers the murder of the suitors. Antinous' father wants revenge, and Odysseus and Telemachus make ready for battle. Athena ultimately orders everyone to stop fighting and peace reigns in Ithaca.

Thought Questions (students consider while they read)

1. Do you believe Telemachus was right to hang the maids for disloyalty?
2. Why do you think Odysseus disguises his identity when he meets his own father?
3. Do you think Antinous' father was right to demand revenge for his son's death?
4. Eurycleia offers to inform on the other maids when she first recognizes Odysseus, but he rejects her offer. Later on, he asks her to do exactly that. Why do you think this is?
5. What do you think about ghostly Agamemnon's response to hearing of Odysseus' slaughter of the suitors?

Vocabulary (in order of appearance)

Book 21:

- lofty: tall, imposing, haughty
- blazing: on fire
- connoisseur: an expert, a tastemaker
- virtuoso: one with great talent

Book 22:

- brandish: to flourish or shake, especially a weapon
- canny: shrewd
- skulk: hide just out of view, lurk

Book 23:

- callous: unfeeling, cruel
- hyacinth: a type of flower

Book 24:

- ambrosia: the food of the gods

Additional Homework

1. Seek out a film or book about a soldier returning from war, such as Hemingway's *The Sun Also Rises*. It's easy to forget that Odysseus has been through a traumatic, many-year war before the *Odyssey* even begins. How do the veterans in other books deal with that trauma differently than Odysseus does? What do these differences tell us about the way that different cultures think of war and soldiering?
2. Research the prominent theories about the poet Homer, which reflect how little information we have about him. Compare the theories and offer evidence for and against each.

Day 5 - Discussion of Thought Questions

1. Do you believe Telemachus was right to hang the maids for disloyalty?

   Time: 5 minutes

   Discussion: This part of the book is really grisly, and this scene in particular shows Odysseus taking his revenge overboard. Students should discuss why the maids are seen as disloyal when the bard and herald who served the suitors are spared because "they had no choice." An exploration of gender double standards would be appropriate here.

2. Why do you think Odysseus disguises his identity when he meets his own father?

   Time: 5 minutes

   Discussion: The characters of the *Odyssey* often test each other's loyalty. Odysseus is particularly paranoid, and has a penchant for disguise and trickery. He decides to "test the old man," presumably to make sure he remains loyal to his son.

3. Do you think Antinous' father was right to demand revenge for his son's death?

   Time: 5 minutes

   Discussion: Obviously it is reasonable for a father to be angry about his son's murder. However, students might also discuss the character of Antinous and his transgressions: Overstaying his welcome, plotting to kill Telemachus, unbearable rudeness and arrogance. There is a case to be made that he got what he deserved.

4. Eurycleia offers to inform on the other maids when she first recognizes Odysseus, but he rejects her offer. Later on, he asks her to do exactly that. Why do you think this is?

   Time: 5 minutes

   Discussion: Students should discuss the pride of Odysseus. He likes to execute his own ideas, rather than following orders. He may also have decided that testing the maids on his own time and in his own way was no longer feasible, so he finally decided to ask for help.

5. What do you think about ghostly Agamemnon's response to hearing of Odysseus' slaughter of the suitors?

   Time: 5 minutes

   Discussion: Agamemnon relates the situation back to Penelope, who is rare among women in that she is trustworthy. He doesn't seem at all taken aback by the horrendous violence, probably reflecting his background as a soldier.

Day 5 - Short Answer Quiz

1. Why did Odysseus leave his bow at home?

___

2. Who does Penelope ask to set the bow?

___

3. How does Odysseus reveal his identity to Eumaeus?

___

4. How does Antinous react when the disguised Odysseus asks to try to string the bow?

___

5. Who is the first of the suitors to die?

___

6. How does Amphinomous die?

___

7. How does the prophet and suitor Leodes die?

---

8. What is Penelope's nickname for Troy?

---

9. Why can't Odysseus and Penelope's bed be moved?

---

10. How does Odysseus initially approach his father?

Short Answer Quiz Key

1. It was of great sentimental value.
2. Eumaeus, the swineherd.
3. Odysseus reveals his leg scar to Eumaeus.
4. With derision and anger.
5. Antinous
6. Telemachus stabs him.
7. He begs Odysseus for mercy and Odysseus hacks his throat with a sword.
8. Destroy
9. It's built around a tree.
10. He pretends to be a total stranger.

Day 5 - Crossword Puzzle

ACROSS

2. The suitors honor ___ to improve their archery
5. A decorative pin
7. The food of the gods
8. Retaliation
13. The king of the gods
15. Odysseus shows this to prove his identity
16. Agamemnon's faithless wife
19. Scavenger birds that eat the dead
20. The suitors try to shoot an arrow through twelve ____

DOWN

1. Odysseus shoots Antinous in the ___
3. The mountain where the gods live
4. A carving tool
6. Who tries to help the suitors and is killed?
9. Odysseus proves his identity to ___
10. Odysseus disguises himself as a ___
11. Who kills the disloyal maids?
12. Odysseus and Penelope's bed was built around a ___ tree
14. Who locks the doors to keep the suitors inside?
17. One who seeks another's hand in marriage
18. A surprise attack

Crossword Puzzle Answer Key

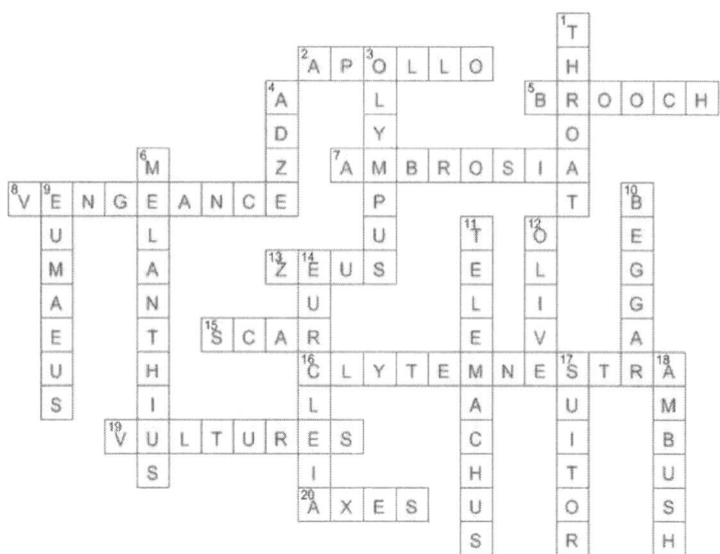

ACROSS

2. The suitors honor ___ to improve their archery
5. A decorative pin
7. The food of the gods
8. Retaliation
13. The king of the gods
15. Odysseus shows this to prove his identity
16. Agamemnon's faithless wife
19. Scavenger birds that eat the dead
20. The suitors try to shoot an arrow through twelve ____

DOWN

1. Odysseus shoots Antinous in the ___
3. The mountain where the gods live
4. A carving tool
6. Who tries to help the suitors and is killed?
9. Odysseus proves his identity to ___
10. Odysseus disguises himself as a ___
11. Who kills the disloyal maids?
12. Odysseus and Penelope's bed was built around a ___ tree
14. Who locks the doors to keep the suitors inside?
17. One who seeks another's hand in marriage
18. A surprise attack

Day 5 - Vocabulary Quiz

Terms	Answers
1. ____ lofty	A. on fire
2. ____ blazing	B. hide just out of view, lurk
3. ____ connoisseur	C. shrewd
4. ____ virtuoso	D. unfeeling, cruel
5. ____ brandish	E. the food of the gods
6. ____ canny	F. one with great talent
7. ____ skulk	G. to flourish or shake, especially a weapon
8. ____ callous	H. a type of flower
9. ____ hyacinth	I. an expert, a tastemaker
10. ____ ambrosia	J. tall, imposing, haughty

Vocabulary Quiz Answer Key

1. J
2. A
3. I
4. F
5. G
6. C
7. B
8. D
9. H
10. E

Day 5 - Classroom Activities

1. Ithacan Trail

Kind of Activity: Mixed Media
Objective: To depict the events of the poem in an interactive way.
Common Core State Standards: CCSS.ELA-Literacy.CCRA.R.7 ; CCSS.ELA-Literacy.CCRA.R.1
Time: 1 hour

Structure:

As a class, look at the layout from Day 4 of the series of events Odysseus encounters on his way home to Ithaca. Then, as a group, work together to create a board game charting Odysseus' journey.

Every major episode must be represented and assigned a function in the game (e.g. "Scylla and Charybdis! If you roll a four or higher, go forward two spaces. If you roll a three or lower, go back three spaces.") The object of the game will be to get back to Ithaca. After playing a few rounds of the game, you can also talk about how games affect our perspective on a story: How does being asked to "play" a specific character enable us to empathize with that person? Is it a deeper empathy than that of merely reading about characters? How does participation in this way affect the way we process information?

Ideans for Differentiated Instruction:

-Assign students to tasks based on their interests and strengths; for instance, visually inclined students can work on the design and layout of the game while others could work out the strategic aspects or write copy for the cards and board spaces.

-Students could work in groups to develop different parts of the game, or each group could develop its own game to share with the class.

-Consider having students create an online game with the same goals.

Assessment Ideas:

-Have students turn in the final board game for evaluation by the instructor.

-Ask students to assess their groupmates in terms of teamwork, leadership, and contributions to the finished product.

2. The Hero's Journey

Kind of Activity: Mixed Media
Objective: To understand Odysseus' travels as part of a literary tradition.
Common Core State Standards: CCSS.ELA-Literacy.CCRA.W.9 ; CCSS.ELA-Literacy.CCRA.R.2
Time: 30 minutes

Structure:

As a class, discuss the concept of Joseph Campbell's Hero's Journey, and the steps that often go into making a narrative such as the Odyssey. Why are these narratives satisfying or exciting? What are the problems with seeing so many stories through this lens? Talk about other examples of the hero's journey in popular culture, such as the stories of Luke Skywalker or Katniss Everdeen.

Working individually, students should prepare a visual project that analyzes the *Odyssey* in terms of the hero's journey and relates it to another hero's journey narrative. You can either assign each student a story, let them choose their own, or prepare a list of options that they can pick from. Make sure they understand each step of Campbell's journey, why it matters and what it means, before they attempt their own analysis of stories.

Ideans for Differentiated Instruction:

-Artistic students could paint or draw their project, while those without a visual bent could create a collage or something less labor-intensive.

-Students could work individually or in small groups.

Assessment Ideas:
-Evaluate the reports/representations for the quality of the research done and the depth of analysis they offer for their chosen story.

Final Paper

Essay Questions

1. Guile and cunning are woven throughout the Odyssey. Is guile considered a virtue or a character flaw? Does this change depending on the character in question? Cite examples from the text to justify your argument.

2. The *Odyssey* was originally delivered orally, as a long story, and storytelling plays a large part in the narrative. Books 9-12 are narrated by Odysseus himself. Do you think Odysseus can be considered a reliable narrator of his own tales? What about the narrator of the story itself?

3. Revenge is ever-present in the *Odyssey*. Consider the different forms this revenge takes and whether it is considered righteous or not.

4. The Odyssey is named after Odysseus, so it is natural to think of him as the hero. Make an argument that Telemachus, not Odysseus, is the main character of the story.

5. Odysseus wants nothing more than to be at home in Ithaca. But do you think now that the story is over, he will be content to stay in Ithaca and be king?

6. There are many women in the *Odyssey*, and many of them are portrayed in a negative light. But one whose portrayal is almost entirely positive is the goddess Athena, who helps Odysseus all along his path. How is Athena's character a contrast to the other female characters in the Odyssey—or is she?

7. Would Odysseus have gotten home a lot faster if he hadn't gotten stuck being a good guest for weeks and months? What does it mean to be a good guest or host in Homer's epic?

Advice on research sources

A. School or community library

Ask your reference librarian for help locating books on the following subjects:

* Greek mythology and legend

* The *Odyssey*

* The Hero's Journey

* Epic poetry

* Religion in the ancient world

* Oral traditions

B. Other literary works

Relevant works include the *Iliad* and works based on the *Odyssey* like James Joyce's *Ulysses*.

Grading rubric for essays

Style:

* words: spelling and diction

* sentences: grammar and punctuation

* paragraphs: organization

* essay: structure

* argument: rhetoric, reasonableness, creativity

Content:

* accuracy

* use of evidence

* addresses the question

* completeness

* uses literary concepts

* addresses complex and sensitive subjects with understanding and nuance

Final Paper Answer Key

Remember that essays about literature should not be graded with a cookie-cutter approach whereby specific words or ideas are required. See the grading rubric above for a variety of criteria to use in assessing answers to the essay questions. This answer key thus functions as a store of ideas for students who need additional guidance in framing their answers.

1. Guile and cunning are woven throughout the Odyssey. Is guile considered a virtue or a character flaw? Does this change depending on the character in question? Cite examples from the text to justify your argument.

   Answers should acknowledge that lying and plotting are clearly considered both good and bad depending on who is doing the lying. For example, Odysseus lies almost compulsively and often without clear reason to everyone he meets (why conceal his identity to his own aged father, for example?), but many women in the story are portrayed as untrustworthy when displaying the same tendencies. Even Penelope, whose guile when deceiving the suitors is celebrated, is automatically considered unreliable merely by virtue of her gender.

2. The *Odyssey* was originally delivered orally, as a long story, and storytelling plays a large part in the narrative. Books 9-12 are narrated by Odysseus himself. Do you think Odysseus can be considered a reliable narrator of his own tales? What about the narrator of the story itself?

   Strong answers will bring up the fact that the narrator of the *Odyssey* editorializes frequently and that part of the point of the epic seems to be the lionization of Odysseus--his actions are described accurately but no matter his behavior, he is seen as a good and heroic man. Responses should discuss the fact that Odysseus lies to almost everyone in the story, so why not to his hosts at Phaeacia? And why not to us? But essays should acknowledge that since this is the only angle from which we know the story, we don't have an alternate or unbiased narrative to guide our thinking.

3. Revenge is ever-present in the *Odyssey*. Consider the different forms this revenge takes and whether it is considered righteous or not.

   Good answers will not only discuss the obvious (the revenge Odysseus enacts on his wife's suitors), but also the revenge taken out on Odysseus by Poseidon, which dogs him throughout the epic. Why is one vendetta considered just and another unjust? Students may bring up the fact that Odysseus takes revenge by killing the suitors, whereas Poseidon intends only to keep Odysseus in misery as long as possible. They may also bring up Poseidon's callous murder of a ship full of Phaeacians, which was a glancing part of his revenge on Odysseus.

4. The Odyssey is named after Odysseus, so it is natural to think of him as the hero. Make an argument that Telemachus, not Odysseus, is the main character of the story.

   Strong answers will focus on the fact that Telemachus changes and comes of age over the course of the Odyssey, and Odysseus stays pretty much the same except for his geographical location. It can be argued that Odysseus' story is merely a vehicle to talk about Telemachus' growth.

5. Odysseus wants nothing more than to be at home in Ithaca. But do you think now that the story is over, he will be content to stay in Ithaca and be king?

   Students answering this question should note Odysseus' craving for adventure and love of a good story. They will probably conclude that life on land won't be to Odysseus' liking, but they may also observe that someone who seems comfortable making up his own exploits can just as easily make them up from shore. This question may work best if students have been encouraged to read Alfred Tennyson's poem "Ulysses," which deals with exactly this situation and portrays Odysseus as bored and restless.

6. There are many women in the *Odyssey*, and many of them are portrayed in a negative light. But one whose portrayal is almost entirely positive is the goddess Athena, who helps Odysseus all along his path. How is Athena's character a contrast to the other female characters in the Odyssey—or is she?

   Answers should acknowledge that many women in the Odyssey who are denigrated by the narrator or the other characters have not actually done anything wrong. Athena is brave and interesting (though she has her own possible weaknesses, like her refusal to really fight Poseidon on the question of Odysseus), and her good qualities are acknowledged. However, the other female characters are assumed to be faithless and silly. Essays may discuss the fact that Athena's affection for Odysseus seems almost romantic at times, so far does it overstep the bounds of admiration between soldiers (as a warrior goddess, Athena is in a way the ultimate soldier).

7. Would Odysseus have gotten home a lot faster if he hadn't gotten stuck being a good guest for weeks and months? What does it mean to be a good guest or host in Homer's epic?

   Good answers will cite specific examples of the power balances being negotiated between host and guest, and chart the differences between kingly hosts and peasant hosts. Is one more generous than the other, given their relative means? Answers should acknowledge that peasants always indicate that they take in travelers because you never know which ones are sent by the gods, so in some ways their bent toward hospitality is a direct result of their fear of their gods.

Final Exam

A. Multiple Choice

Circle the letter corresponding to the best answer.

1. Which god looks after Odysseus?

   (A) Poseidon
   (B) Hephaestus
   (C) Aphrodite
   (D) Athena

2. Whose cattle should Odysseus' men not have eaten?

   (A) Zeus
   (B) Nestor
   (C) Helios
   (D) Menelaus

3. How did Agamemnon die?

   (A) He is still alive
   (B) He was killed by his wife's lover Aegisthus
   (C) He died fighting in the Trojan War
   (D) Odysseus killed him in a quarrel

4. What does Circe change Odysseus' men into?

   (A) Bigger men
   (B) Bears
   (C) Cattle
   (D) Pigs

5. Which ghost refuses to speak to Odysseus?

   (A) Clytemnestra
   (B) Leda
   (C) Achilles
   (D) Ajax

6. Who is Polyphemus' father?

(A) Zeus
(B) Poseidon
(C) Odysseus
(D) Proteus

7. Why does Telemachus leave Ithaca?

(A) His mother threatens to kill him
(B) He wants to make a name for himself as a sailor
(C) Athena tells him to
(D) He doesn't have any friends

8. What happened to Odysseus' mother?

(A) She became a nun
(B) She was killed by the suitors
(C) She became a sea captain
(D) She died of grief

9. Which of these men is alive in The Odyssey?

(A) Menelaus
(B) Agamemnon
(C) Priam
(D) Achilles

10. Who is Pisistratus?

(A) The captain of the Phaeacian ship
(B) The King of the Underworld
(C) The son of Nestor
(D) The father of Odysseus

11. Who is Odysseus looking for in Hades?

(A) Telemachus
(B) Tiresias
(C) Laertes
(D) Orestes

12. Why doesn't Nausicaa bring Odysseus back to her father's palace directly?

(A) Because her father is missing
(B) To avoid gossip
(C) Because there is no room in her carriage
(D) Because she hates him

13. Which woman is ostensibly the cause of the Trojan War?

(A) Helen
(B) Eurycleia
(C) Calypso
(D) Penelope

14. Who is Alcinous?

(A) King of the Phaeacians
(B) King of the Spartans
(C) a loyal swineherd
(D) King of the Britons

15. How does the narrator often refer to Odysseus?

(A) "Man of ice and fire"
(B) "Man of guts and glory"
(C) "Man of strong opinions"
(D) "Man of twists and turns"

16. When is the Odyssey set?

(A) During the Seafaring Age
(B) During the Gold Age
(C) During the Iron Age
(D) During the Bronze Age

17. What is Scylla?

(A) A magic sword
(B) Charybdis' wife
(C) A sea monster
(D) A river goddess

18. What does Odysseus sacrifice in order to speak to the dead?

(A) His left ear
(B) His memories of his wife
(C) Some sheep
(D) A sailor who is his friend

19. Why does Calypso let Odysseus go?

(A) He is dying of grief
(B) Zeus tells her to
(C) She gets bored of him
(D) She falls in love with someone else

20. Who does Odysseus tell his true identity to?

(A) Laertes
(B) Eumaeus
(C) Athena
(D) King Antinous

B. Short Answer

1. How does Odysseus identify himself to Polyphemus?

___

2. Who did Agamemnon bring back with him from the Trojan War?

___

3. Which two characters tell Odysseus not to eat the cattle of the sun?

___

4. Whose house does Telemachus visit first upon returning to Ithaca?

___

5. Why are the Sirens dangerous?

___

6. What is moly?

___

7. What kind of animal does Polyphemus raise?

___

8. Why is Odysseus embarrassed when he meets Nausicaa?

____

9. How does Odysseus' nurse recognize him when he returns?

____

10. How does Penelope make her suitors compete?

____

C. Vocabulary

Terms	Answers
1. ____ lyre	A. stranded on an island
2. ____ marooned	B. ancient stringed instrument similar to a harp
3. ____ Muse	C. horrible, disgusting
4. ____ swell	D. a fortification, a wall built for defense
5. ____ bulwark	E. a drink poured out to honor a god
6. ____ flitter	F. Goddess of inspiration, one of nine, each representing a different art.
7. ____ grisly	G. chaos
8. ____ pyre	H. a mound of flammable material, often used for burning dead bodies in a funeral rite
9. ____ libation	I. a sea wave that never breaks
10. ____ pandemonium	J. to move quickly but without purpose

D. Short Essays

1. Consider the idea that Odysseus might be a pawn in a game between Athena and Poseidon. Do you agree or disagree? Support your argument with evidence from the text.

2. After Odysseus arrives in Ithaca, the story becomes somewhat repetitive until its climax. How does Homer keep the dramatic tension going, even though very little happens?

3. Do you think Penelope is as cunning as Odysseus? Offer examples to support your opinion.

Final Exam Answer Key

A. Multiple Choice Answer Key

1. D
2. C
3. B
4. D
5. D
6. B
7. C
8. D
9. A
10. C
11. B
12. B
13. A
14. A
15. D
16. D
17. C
18. C
19. B
20. D

B. Short Answer Key

1. As "Nobody" or "No man"
2. Princess Cassandra, the cursed prophetess.
3. Circe and Tiresias.
4. Eumaeus
5. They sing a song so beautiful that it lures sailors to their deaths on treacherous rocks.
6. A drug, given to Odysseus by Hermes, that makes him impervious to Circe's witchcraft.
7. Sheep.
8. He's naked.
9. By the scar on his leg.
10. In an archery competition using Odysseus' bow.

C. Vocabulary Answer Key

1. B
2. A
3. F
4. I
5. D
6. J
7. C
8. H
9. E
10. G

D. Short Essays Answer Key

1. It is possible to argue in favor of this idea, but most students will probably argue against. Odysseus displays too much free will, guile and cunning to seem like a pawn for anyone, and, while Athena and some other gods help him, he definitely has to struggle to stay alive.
2. Answers should focus on the fact that Odysseus is constantly in danger of being found out, and that people keep commenting on how like Odysseus he is. He is even recognized at one point (by the nurse who washes his feet), but he convinces her to stay silent. The reader knows that once Odysseus is found out, he'll have to start wreaking real havoc, so the plot hovers in stasis for several books, with the omens piling up and the suitors becoming ever more unbearable.
3. It is difficult to argue this on a level playing field—Odysseus has so many more adventures and lies to literally everyone, because he has the luxury of disguise to do so. But Penelope's ruse with the shroud-weaving is clear evidence of her guile, which she uses in ways that are specifically tied to the home and traditionally feminine tasks.

Table of Contents

Table of Contents

Table of Contents

Table of Contents

Teaching Guide - About the Author

The ancient Greeks hailed Homer as their greatest poet. Although the Greeks recognized other poets who composed in Greek before Homer, no texts from these earlier poets survived. Perhaps they were lost, or perhaps they were never written down. Homer himself was probably on the cusp between the tradition of oral poetry and the new invention of written language. Texts of the *Iliad* and the *Odyssey* existed from at least the sixth century BCE, and probably for a considerable span of time before that. These two great epic poems also had a life in performance: through the centuries, professional artists made their living by reciting Homer, performing the great epics for audiences that often know great parts of the poem by heart.

It is impossible to pin down with any certainty when (or if) Homer lived. Eratosthenes gives the traditional date of 1184 BC for the end of the Trojan War, the semi-mythical event which forms the basis for the Iliad. The great Greek historian Herodotus put the date at 1250 BCE. These dates were arrived at in a very approximate manner; Greek historians usually used genealogy and estimation when trying to find the dates for events in the distant past. But Greek historians were far less certain about the dates for Homer's life. Some said he was a contemporary of the events of the *Iliad*, while others placed him sixty or a hundred or several hundred years afterward. Herodotus estimated that Homer lived and wrote in the ninth century BCE. He almost certainly lived in one of the Greek city-states in Asia Minor. All of the traditional sources say that he was blind.

Over the course of millennia of scholarly speculation, prevailing theories about Homer and his relationship to his work have had time to change and change again. At various times over the centuries, scholars have suggested that he was only a transmitter, or that he never existed, and the epics attributed to him were the patchwork effort of generations of bards. Most modern scholars, however, hold that Homer was a great bard who lived between the eighth and seventh centuries BCE. Although there is little doubt that Homer inherited a massive amount of material from generations of bards before him, most scholars believe now that Homer was an innovator and an original artist as well as a transmitter. Writing probably played a role in the composition of his great poems. Current theories depict Homer as a master of oral poetry who used the new invention of writing to aid him in composing epics on a grander scale than had ever been done before.

Little can be known with certainty. But even though the details of Homer's life are elusive, his works have formed a foundation for all the Western literature that has followed, and his characters and stories have had an impact on three thousand years' worth of readers.

Teaching Guide - Study Objectives

If all of the elements of this lesson plan are employed, students will develop the following powers, skills, and understanding:

1. Have a basic understanding of Greek mythology and legend, and its influence on world culture and storytelling.

2. Be able to identify the markers of epic poetry and be comfortable with texts that use it.

3. Make nuanced arguments about the literary and popular concept of the hero.

4. Be comfortable identifying clear symbols in texts.

Teaching Guide - Common Core Standards

- 9-10 - CCSS.ELA-Literacy.CCRA.W.1 Write arguments to support claims in an analysis of substantive topics or texts using valid reasoning and relevant and sufficient evidence.

- 9-10 - CCSS.ELA-Literacy.CCRA.W.2 Write informative/explanatory texts to examine and convey complex ideas and information clearly and accurately through the effective selection, organization, and analysis of content.

- 9-10 - CCSS.ELA-Literacy.CCRA.W.3 Write narratives to develop real or imagined experiences or events using effective technique, well-chosen details and well-structured event sequences.

- 9-10 - CCSS.ELA-Literacy.CCRA.W.5 Develop and strengthen writing as needed by planning, revising, editing, rewriting, or trying a new approach.

- 9-10 - CCSS.ELA-Literacy.CCRA.W.9 Draw evidence from literary or informational texts to support analysis, reflection, and research.

- 9-10 - CCSS.ELA-Literacy.CCRA.R.1 Read closely to determine what the text says explicitly and to make logical inferences from it; cite specific textual evidence when writing or speaking to support conclusions drawn from the text.

- 9-10 - CCSS.ELA-Literacy.CCRA.R.2 Determine central ideas or themes of a text and analyze their development; summarize the key supporting details and ideas.

- 9-10 - CCSS.ELA-Literacy.CCRA.R.3 Analyze how and why individuals, events, or ideas develop and interact over the course of a text.

- 9-10 - CCSS.ELA-Literacy.CCRA.R.4 Interpret words and phrases as they are used in a text, including determining technical, connotative, and figurative meanings, and analyze how specific word choices shape meaning or tone.

- 9-10 - CCSS.ELA-Literacy.CCRA.R.5 Analyze the structure of texts, including how specific sentences, paragraphs, and larger portions of the text (e.g., a section, chapter, scene, or stanza) relate to each other and the whole.

- 9-10 - CCSS.ELA-Literacy.CCRA.R.7 Integrate and evaluate content presented in diverse media and formats, including visually and quantitatively, as well as in words.

- 9-10 - CCSS.ELA-Literacy.CCRA.SL.1 Prepare for and participate effectively in a range of conversations and collaborations with diverse partners, building on others' ideas and expressing their own clearly and persuasively.

- 9-10 - CCSS.ELA-Literacy.CCRA.SL.3 Evaluate a speaker's point of view, reasoning, and use of evidence and rhetoric.

- 9-10 - CCSS.ELA-Literacy.CCRA.SL.4 Present information, findings, and supporting evidence such that listeners can follow the line of reasoning and the organization, development, and style are appropriate to task, purpose, and audience.

Teaching Guide - Introduction to The Odyssey

The epics of the ancient Greek bard Homer are long poems that preserve myths and legends in verse and were almost certainly delivered orally before they were written down. They take the form of poetry, in fact, because rhyming text is much easier to memorize and deliver than prose. The *Odyssey* describes Odysseus' journey home to Ithaca after the fall of Troy. The *Odyssey* is so important to Western literature that its title has become a noun meaning "a journey," usually with the connotation of detour and adventure along the way.

Key Aspects of The Odyssey

Tone

The *Odyssey*'s tone stands in stark contrast to that of the *Iliad*. While the first story is full of gore and glory, the *Odyssey* takes more time for comedy and pays more attention to silly details, without abandoning the heroic tone he took when describing the exploits of heroes in the *Iliad*.

Setting

The *Odyssey* takes place over the course of ten years, and it is a constant journey from island to island, adventure to adventure. The only real constant setting is back in Ithaca, where Odysseus' wife tries to deal with her unruly suitors while waiting for her husband to show up, but that is a minor part of the book when compared to the various adventures had by Odysseus and his son Telemachus on their separate journeys.

Point of View

The *Odyssey* has a third-person narrator, as is clear from the opening words of the poem: "Sing to me of the man, Muse, the man of twists and turns." The whole story (with a diversion for a few books where Odysseus becomes the narrator) is told by an omniscient speaker, which adds to the sense of the book as something like a theatrical performance.

Character Development

Odysseus is the hero of the piece, but his character stays relatively static. He is brave, lucky, very clever, and very proud. He trusts nobody and often lies about his own identity, just in case someone else is trying to trick him. His objective throughout the poem is returning safely to Ithaca and his wife Penelope.

Penelope is the perfect wife—beautiful, good at household tasks like weaving, and she cries all the time. But she's also the perfect wife for Odysseus, in that she's wily, strong, smart, and unendingly loyal. Her character is very stable, which it has to be since she symbolizes home to Odysseus.

Telemachus, Odysseus' son, is the only character who develops. He starts out despairing and entitled—he hates his life but feels he can't change it; he is rude to his mother and angry about his father's apparent death in anonymity and not at Troy in a blaze of glory. However, once he has hope of seeing his father again, he begins to find his strength and courage, and when he and Odysseus fight side by side he comes into his own as a man.

Themes

Disguise — Odysseus is constantly either disguising his own identity by lying to people, or being disguised via the work of the goddess Athena. Athena also disguises herself in myriad ways in order to appear to humans. Disguise creates the major suspense in the latter half of the poem, as it is unclear when and how Odysseus will reveal his true identity once in Ithaca.

Revenge — Odysseus' revenge on the suitors is the most obvious instance of this theme, but Telemachus desires revenge from the book's outset, and Poseidon's revenge on Odysseus drives much of his wandering.

Hospitality — Since the book concerns traveling, almost everyone in it acts as either host or guest. Hospitality emerges as the main signifier of morality, in fact. If you are a good guest or host, you are a good person and will be rewarded, unless you are a Phaeacian sailor.

The Faithfulness/Faithlessness of Women — Everyone in the *Odyssey* is very concerned with whether Penelope, as a woman, can be trusted. Women are constantly portrayed as evil or at least as temptresses, except Penelope, who is cast as one against her will in some cases, but whose selflessness and true loyalty never waver.

Symbols

The Bed - Odysseus and Penelope's wedding bed symbolizes their marriage and the home that he is struggling to return to. It is immovable (built around a tree) and was handmade by Odysseus himself.

The Bow — Odysseus' great bow cannot be lifted or strung by lesser men. When the suitors try, they prove how physically inferior they are to Odysseus and how they literally cannot take his place. Telemachus also fails to string the bow, but the narrator intimates that he probably could have succeeded had he tried again.

Clothing — Clothes were difficult and expensive to make in ancient Greece, so when a traveler is given clothes in the poem, that is a sign of great respect, hospitality and acceptance.

Climax

The climax of the story arrives when Odysseus throws off his disguise and slaughters his wife's suitors en masse, winding up covered with blood in his own great hall.

Structure

The *Odyssey* is divided into 24 books. The original poem is a little over 12,000 lines, making it significantly shorter than the *Iliad*.

Teaching Guide - Relationship with Other Books

One cannot discuss the *Odyssey* without discussing its companion, the *Iliad*. The *Iliad*, which was probably written first and takes place directly before the *Odyssey*, is a graphic, violent epic about a massive war and siege. The *Odyssey*, by contrast, is almost a comic epic, an adventure of a man trying to get home to see his family. It's also key to remember that the *Odyssey* is a love story, in contrast to the *Iliad* which depicts a war.

The *Odyssey* has inspired many other works of art — the most obvious is James Joyce's *Ulysses*, but students who aren't quite up for that might enjoy the Coen Brothers' film *O Brother, Where Art Thou*, or Margaret Atwood's short retelling of the story from the point of view of Odysseus' wife, *The Penelopiad*. Alfred, Lord Tennyson's poem "Ulysses" is also based on the *Odyssey*.

Also consider other books chronicling episodic journeys, like Voltaire's *Candide*.

Teaching Guide - Bringing In Technology

For presentations and artistic responses, offer students the option of powerpoint or video in addition a standard presentation. For the board game activity, consider creating an online game with the same general characteristics.

Because the *Odyssey* is necessarily read in translation, an audiobook would be a useful resource--perhaps the version of the Robert Fagles translation read by Ian McKellen.

Another resource that could be of use is "O Brother, Where Art Thou," a loose film adaptation of the *Odyssey* set in the Depression-era Deep South. The film might encourage students put off by the language and exoticism of Homer to open up to the text.

There is an Android app that recreates the *Odyssey* as an adventure game that students may enjoy playing through.

Teaching Guide - Notes to the Teacher

Poetry is difficult to teach in translation. Editions that try to preserve Homer's famous dactylic hexameter often sacrifice meaning or clarity in service of the meter. Try to choose a translation, such as the one by Robert Fagles, that preserves meter, flow, and mood, but is perhaps less faithful to the text on a word-for-word basis.

The thought questions in this lesson plan provide material and ideas that students can use to write short original essays and to develop their powers of thought. For the sake of improving the power of expression, teachers should encourage students to write on topics that have been discussed in class, this time in the more formal writing style expected in a literary essay. At the same time, students should not be discouraged from choosing their own topics. The questions provided for the final paper are most suitable for student essays. Remember that grading an essay should not depend on a simple checklist of required content.

Author of Lesson Plan and Sources

Fiona Zublin, author of Lesson Plan. Completed on February 24, 2014, copyright held by GradeSaver.

Updated and revised Michelle Rosenberg March 02, 2014. Copyright held by GradeSaver.

Homer. Trans. Robert Fagles. The Odyssey. New York: Viking, 1996.

Ed. Beth Cohen. The Distaff Side: Representing the Female in Homer's Odyssey. New York: Oxford University Press, 1995.

Ed. M.F. Lindemans. "Encyclopedia Mythica." 2014-01-15. <http://www.pantheon.org/>.

O Brother, Where Art Thou? Dir. Joel and Ethan Coen. Buena Vista Pictures, 2000.

Tennyson, Alfred. "Ulysses." The Charge of the Light Brigade and Other Poems. Ed. Stanley Appelbaum. New York: Dover Publications, 1992.

Related Links

http://www.pantheon.org/areas/mythology/europe/greek/
Encyclopedia Mythica A wealth of information on Greek mythology and legend that should provide adequate background.

http://www.pbs.org/newshour/bb/entertainment/jan-june97/odyssey_3-3.html
Robert Fagles on PBS An interview with the translator and scholar about The Odyssey's lasting impact on Western culture.

http://www.googlelittrips.com/GoogleLit/9-12/Entries/2006/9/15_The_Odyssey_by_Homer.ht
The Odyssey, Mapped An account of some of the scholarly disagreement about the locations mentioned in the Odyssey, and an attempt to map them.

http://www.pitt.edu/~edfloyd/oralhomer.html
Homeric Epithets A little bit more explanation of dactylic hexameter and the use of Homeric epithets.

http://www.laphamsquarterly.org/voices-in-time/not-too-late-to-seek-a-newer-world.php
"Ulysses" The text of Alfred Tennyson's poem imagining Odysseus after his adventures end.

Day 1 - Reading Assignment

Read Books 1-4

Common Core Objectives

- CCSS.ELA-Literacy.CCRA.W.1 Write arguments to support claims in an analysis of substantive topics or texts using valid reasoning and relevant and sufficient evidence.
- CCSS.ELA-Literacy.CCRA.W.2 Write informative/explanatory texts to examine and convey complex ideas and information clearly and accurately through the effective selection, organization, and analysis of content.
- CCSS.ELA-Literacy.CCRA.R.4 Interpret words and phrases as they are used in a text, including determining technical, connotative, and figurative meanings, and analyze how specific word choices shape meaning or tone.
- CCSS.ELA-Literacy.CCRA.L.3 Apply knowledge of language to understand how language functions in different contexts, to make effective choices for meaning or style, and to comprehend more fully when reading or listening.

Note that it is perfectly fine to expand any day's work into two days depending on the characteristics of the class, particularly if the class will engage in all of the suggested classroom exercises and activities and discuss all of the thought questions.

Content Summary for Teachers

Book 1: This first chapter introduces Odysseus and the basic premise: Our hero, Odysseus, has been trying to get home from the Trojan War for years, but unfortunately, he has been cursed by Poseidon (who is angry at Odysseus for killing his son, the cyclops Polyphemus). While Poseidon is off receiving offerings at a feast in Ethiopia, the other gods discuss the situation. Athena appeals to her father, Zeus, on Odysseus' behalf. They agree to send messenger god Hermes to Calypso and tell her to let Odysseus go, while Athena herself visits Odysseus' son Telemachus. She disguises herself as a human nobleman, Mentes, and goes to Odysseus' estate in Ithaca. There she finds a horde of suitors who all want to marry Odysseus' wife, Penelope (who remains faithful to Odysseus). Athena urges Telemachus to go on a sea voyage and look for news of his father. After an interlude where a bard plays a song that makes Penelope cry, Telemachus angrily throws all the suitors out of the house.

Book 2: Telemachus calls a council of Ithaca's elders. He explains that the suitors are eating him out of house and home, but that Penelope has devised a scheme to deter them, claiming that she cannot marry until she has finished weaving a shroud for her father in law: she weaves all day but secretly unravels all her work at night. Telemachus says that if the suitors don't leave, he will call on the wrath of Zeus. To show his support, Zeus releases two eagles. The noblemen argue about the meaning of the sign, and Telemachus says he plans to go to sea (as Athena advised) to try to find out what happened to his father. He prays to Athena, who again urges him to voyage and tells him to leave in secret. He goes about putting together the expedition, begging for help from his nurse, whom he swears to secrecy. Athena, meanwhile, gets the suitors intoxicated so they won't notice Telemachus leaving. He and his friends set sail, with Athena at the helm.

Book 3: Telemachus and Athena sail to Pylos, where King Nestor reigns. Nestor fought in the Trojan War alongside Odysseus. Telemachus asks Nestor if he knows anything about Odysseus' whereabouts or fate. Nestor tells him about the end of the war, when Menelaus wanted everyone to sail home (which Nestor did) and Agamemnon wanted everyone to stay and fight (which Odysseus eventually did). Still, Nestor does't know anything about Odysseus' fate. Nestor advises Telemachus to visit Menelaus next, but invites them to stay the night. Telemachus agrees, and Athena says she should go back to the ship for the night, whereupon she flies away in eagle form and Nestor realizes she's a goddess. They sacrifice a cow in her honor.

Book 4:

Telemachus and Athena, with Nestor's son Pisistratus, sail to Lacedaemon, where Menelaus rules with his queen Helen. The men reminisce about the war and become nostalgic and sad, so Helen drugs their wine with something that keeps them from crying and then reminisces about the war herself to entertain them. The next day, Telemachus explains his situation and asks Menelaus for news of his father. Menelaus tells how he captured Proteus, who told him of Agamemnon's death and of Odysseus' capture by the nymph Calypso.

Back in Ithaca, the suitors discover that Telemachus has left. Furious, they decide to ambush his ship and kill him when he returns. Penelope is devastated by the news that her son has gone, and she prays to Athena to keep him safe. Later that night Athena visits Penelope and tells her not to worry about Telemachus, but refuses to give her any information about Odysseus himself.

Thought Questions (students consider while they read)

1. Though the story is about Odysseus, we're close to one quarter of the way through the story and he hasn't appeared or spoken a line. We only hear other people's stories about him. How does that emphasize the themes of myth and storytelling already prominent in The Odyssey?
2. Telemachus is praised as a hero by everyone who meets him. But he doesn't always treat his mother very respectfully. Do you think this reflects the role of women in Greek society?

3. The Greek gods aren't all-powerful and they're not always particularly just. How do you think having this pantheon of superbeings, who often fight or disagree with each other, affects the world of the characters in The Odyssey?
4. Telemachus acts as both a host (to Athena) and a guest (to Nestor and Menelaus). How do concepts of hospitality in ancient Greece differ from the ones you're used to today, and why do you think that is?
5. As Telemachus journeys around Greece, people often feel like they know him because they assume he must be like his father—a man who Telemachus barely knows. How does the poem approach this idea of men being judged by the characters of their fathers?

Vocabulary (in order of appearance)

Book 1:

- Muse: Goddess of inspiration, one of nine, each representing a different art.
- hallowed: Holy
- Atlas: Titan who holds the world on his shoulders
- decree: order or edict
- staid: traditional, respectable, unexciting
- swagger: walk confidently
- lyre: ancient stringed instrument similar to a harp
- distaff: a tool used when spinning wool by hand

Book 2:

- scepter: a ceremonial staff or stick held by a king, a symbol of rule
- pinions: the feathers at the edge of a bird's wing
- rabble: a mob, the masses

Book 3:

- marooned: stranded on an island

Book 4:

- exploits: deeds, adventures

Additional Homework

1. Researching the background of *The Iliad* is very useful for anyone undertaking *The Odyssey*. Students could independently research characters who appear in *The Odyssey* and recall the events of *The Iliad*, like Helen, Nestor, and Menelaus. How have these characters changed in the many

years since they were fighting the Trojan War?

2. The people of Ithaca are concerned with omens, which they think will inform them of the plans and desires of the gods. Research ancient methods of fortune-telling, like looking at bird entrails. Why was it so important to the Greeks to divine the desires of the gods? Write a paragraph or two.

Day 1 - Discussion of Thought Questions

1. Though the story is about Odysseus, we're close to one quarter of the way through the story and he hasn't appeared or spoken a line. We only hear other people's stories about him. How does that emphasize the themes of myth and storytelling already prominent in The Odyssey?

   Time: 5 minutes

   Discussion: The Odyssey is the story of a great hero, but while everyone who talks about Odysseus has only praise for him, as the story continues some of his actions will be much more questionable to a modern audience. Students might discuss how mythologizing a man demolishes his flaws and makes him an unequivocal hero, while keeping in mind that when Menelaus talks of Odysseus, he is in some ways praising him for being so wily and deceitful.

2. Telemachus is praised as a hero by everyone who meets him. But he doesn't always treat his mother very respectfully. Do you think this reflects the role of women in Greek society?

   Time: 5 minutes

   Discussion: It's important to recognize that women were objectified and commodified in ancient Greece, but is also probably worth exploring the idea that Telemachus is to some extent just a grouchy, entitled teenager. This is a question that teenagers reading the Odyssey can relate to their own relationships with their parents.

3. The Greek gods aren't all-powerful and they're not always particularly just. How do you think having this pantheon of superbeings, who often fight or disagree with each other, affects the world of the characters in The Odyssey?

   Time: 10 minutes

Discussion: Though modern religions often teach of a loving or just god, that doesn't seem to be a priority for the Greek deities. Discussion should note that the Greek gods reflect the attitudes and foibles common to humans, rather than the perfect of our inherent flaws. Having many gods means that you have a lot of opportunities for divine protection, but also a lot of opportunities to offend someone. There is a sense that even heroes are caught up in the arguments and machinations of a system they don't understand and can't control.

4. Telemachus acts as both a host (to Athena) and a guest (to Nestor and Menelaus). How do concepts of hospitality in ancient Greece differ from the ones you're used to today, and why do you think that is?

   Time: 5 minutes

   Discussion: The peril of the ancient world may have led to increased emphasis on hospitality, given the hardscrabble nature of life. There's also the fact that in the world of the Odyssey, any unknown guest might be a disguised god. Students familiar with the Bible might draw parallels to hospitality stories from Genesis or Exodus. Also note that it is possible, as in the case of the suitors, for guests to overstay their welcomes. The suitors display the worst qualities any guest could as they actively try to murder their host.

5. As Telemachus journeys around Greece, people often feel like they know him because they assume he must be like his father—a man who Telemachus barely knows. How does the poem approach this idea of men being judged by the characters of their fathers?

   Time: 5 minutes

   Discussion: In this case, it works out well for Telemachus. Everyone loves him because they all love Odysseus. But Odysseus is a man of many flaws, and so is Telemachus. Even Telemachus rages against his father in Book One, saying he wishes Odysseus had died in glory instead of being forgotten; Telemachus even says he isn't sure that Odysseus is his father. As he discovers how well Odysseus is remembered, though, Telemachus seems to reclaim him and take his place in the family.

Day 1 - Short Answer Quiz

1. Why does Athena go to Ithaca?

2. Why is Poseidon angry with Odysseus?

3. Why have all the local noblemen invaded Penelope and Telemachus' house?

4. How did Penelope put off her suitors for three years?

5. Who is Proteus?

6. How did Helen almost ruin Odysseus' plan to infiltrate the city of Troy with a wooden horse?

7. How does Athena soothe Penelope's fears about Telemachus?

8. Who is Antinous?

9. How do Nestor and his household figure out that the disguised Athena is a goddess?

10. How does Helen know Telemachus is Odysseus' son?

Short Answer Quiz Key

1. To let Telemachus know his father is alive.
2. Odysseus killed Poseidon's son Polyphemus, the Cyclops.
3. They are hoping to marry Penelope.
4. By saying she needed to finish weaving a shroud for her father-in-law, and then unraveling each day's work at night.
5. The Old Man of the Sea who tells Menelaus that Odysseus is not dead.
6. She walked around the base of the horse exclaiming the names of the Greek fighters and hoping they would call out in homesickness.
7. She appears to Penelope as a phantom to tell her that Telemachus will be all right.
8. One of Penelope's suitors, who spearheads the plan to ambush and kill Telemachus.
9. She turns into an eagle in front of them.
10. They look exactly alike.

Day 1 - Crossword Puzzle

ACROSS

1. What's the name of the Odyssey's companion book/prequel?
4. What is the Old Man of the Sea's real name?
6. What bird does Zeus send to indicate his support of Telemachus?
7. Who killed Agamemnon?
8. Which great hero led the Myrmidons?
11. What animal does Nestor sacrifice to Athena?
14. Large celebratory formal meal
15. Which nymph is keeping Odysseus captive when the story begins?
16. Making merry, often in a loud or obnoxious fashion
19. A horse drawn vehicle used in ancient warfare
20. The wife of Menelaus

DOWN

2. The goddess who pleads Odysseus' case to Zeus
3. The goddesses of vengeance
5. Which king do Athena and Telemachus visit first?
9. Who was Penelope weaving a shroud for?
10. A court musician and poet
12. A drink used as an offering to a god
13. The personification of inspiration
17. "Dawn with her ___-red fingers"
18. What color are Athena's eyes?

Crossword Puzzle Answer Key

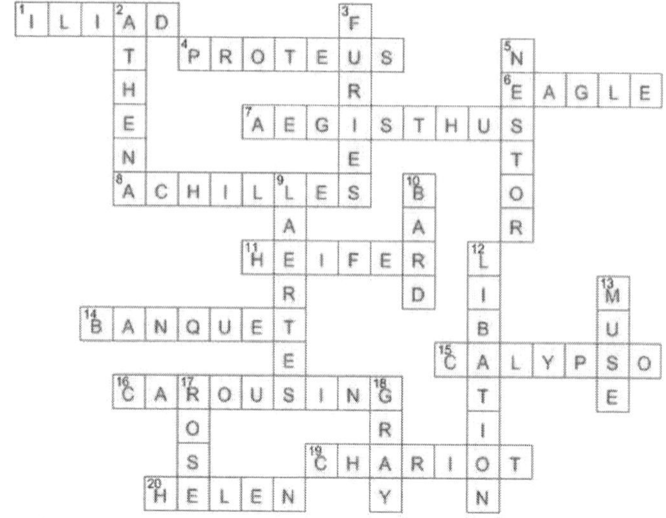

ACROSS

1. What's the name of the Odyssey's companion book/prequel?
4. What is the Old Man of the Sea's real name?
6. What bird does Zeus send to indicate his support of Telemachus?
7. Who killed Agamemnon?
8. Which great hero led the Myrmidons?
11. What animal does Nestor sacrifice to Athena?
14. Large celebratory formal meal
15. Which nymph is keeping Odysseus captive when the story begins?
16. Making merry, often in a loud or obnoxious fashion
19. A horse drawn vehicle used in ancient warfare
20. The wife of Menelaus

DOWN

2. The goddess who pleads Odysseus' case to Zeus
3. The goddesses of vengeance
5. Which king do Athena and Telemachus visit first?
9. Who was Penelope weaving a shroud for?
10. A court musician and poet
12. A drink used as an offering to a god
13. The personification of inspiration
17. "Dawn with her ____-red fingers"
18. What color are Athena's eyes?

Day 1 - Vocabulary Quiz

Terms	Answers
1. ____ Muse	A. stranded on an island
2. ____ hallowed	B. order or edict
3. ____ Atlas	C. holy
4. ____ decree	D. traditional, respectable, unexciting
5. ____ staid	E. a mob, the masses
6. ____ swagger	F. deeds, adventures
7. ____ lyre	G. a ceremonial staff or stick held by a king, a symbol of rule
8. ____ distaff	H. walk confidently
9. ____ scepter	I. a tool used when spinning wool by hand
10. ____ pinions	J. Titan who holds the world on his shoulders
11. ____ rabble	K. ancient stringed instrument similar to a harp
12. ____ marooned	L. the feathers at the edge of a bird's wing
13. ____ exploits	M. Goddess of inspiration, one of nine, each representing a different art.

Vocabulary Quiz Answer Key

1. M
2. C
3. J
4. B
5. D
6. H
7. K
8. I
9. G
10. L
11. E
12. A
13. F

Day 1 - Classroom Activities

1. Myth Masters

Kind of Activity: Research
Objective: To understand the importance of mythology today in relation to its importance in the ancient world
Common Core State Standards: CCSS.ELA-Literacy.CCRA.W.1; CCSS.ELA-Literacy.CCRA.W.2
Time: 45 minutes

Structure:

Separate the students into small groups. Each group should come up with a modern myth that they view as important to their own culture or to life in general. Task them with summarizing the myth and analyzing its cultural importance in preparation for a class presentation.

Once they have summarized their chosen myth, have the students research classical myths that might teach similar lessons or have similar morals or themes. If they can't find anything similar enough, have them choose a contrasting myth or one that relates to theirs in some other, perhaps less obvious, way. Give the students various resources for their research, including books, Internet-enabled devices, and perhaps short audio recordings of mythological stories.

Ask each group to summarize their findings for the class in an informal presentation, and then facilitate a class-wide discussion about each group's findings and presentation.

This activity can be expanded into two days.

Ideans for Differentiated Instruction:

-Consider giving students the option to work individually or in a group.

-Provide different types of resources (for instance, text, audio, video, and interactive websites) for student research.

Assessment Ideas:

-Have students hand in their notes and other presentation materials for evaluation by the instructor.

-Evaluate the student presentations in terms of depth of analysis, quality of research, and ability to convey ideas and support them with evidence.

2. Epithet Experiment

Kind of Activity: Classwide Discussion
Objective: To gain understanding of the structure of Homer's Odyssey
Common Core State Standards: CCSS.ELA-Literacy.CCRA.L.3 ; CCSS.ELA-Literacy.CCRA.R.4
Time: 30 minutes

Structure:

Discuss the concept of Homeric epithets, which are peppered throughout the text of the Odyssey. Get students to list examples, and explain that such repeated epithets (like "man of twists and turns") exist because a lengthy oral epic was hard to remember and the rhythmic structure of *The Odyssey* would be difficult to maintain without repeated lines that could be used where needed. As a class, analyze the importance of the various epithets in the poem ("man of twists and turns" might give more insight into character than "with the lovely braids").

Next, ask students to come up with their own epithets, either for characters in the poem or for characters in other texts that they are familiar with. Have students volunteer for dramatic readings of parts of the text where they replace the original epithets with those generated by the class. Then discuss how the text is different without the original epithets--what makes them work? What makes a good or effective epithet?

Ideans for Differentiated Instruction:

-Students could split into groups to come up with epithets, so that more advanced students can help those who are struggling.

-For students who are less familiar with the concept of epithets, consider providing a variety of nouns and adjectives to choose from.

Assessment Ideas:

-Assess how well the students engage with the text during the class discussion, and how they respond to questions about their epithets or ideas for epithets.

-Have students turn in their lists to the instructor for evaluation.

Day 2 - Reading Assignment

Book 5-10

Common Core Objectives

- CCSS.ELA-Literacy.CCRA.R.3 Analyze how and why individuals, events, or ideas develop and interact over the course of a text.
- CCSS.ELA-Literacy.CCRA.SL.4 Present information, findings, and supporting evidence such that listeners can follow the line of reasoning and the organization, development, and style are appropriate to task, purpose, and audience.
- CCSS.ELA-Literacy.CCRA.SL.3 Evaluate a speaker's point of view, reasoning, and use of evidence and rhetoric.
- CCSS.ELA-Literacy.CCRA.SL.1 Prepare for and participate effectively in a range of conversations and collaborations with diverse partners, building on others' ideas and expressing their own clearly and persuasively.

Note that it is perfectly fine to expand any day's work into two days depending on the characteristics of the class, particularly if the class will engage in all of the suggested classroom exercises and activities and discuss all of the thought questions.

Content Summary for Teachers

Book 5: At another gathering of the gods, Zeus orders Hermes to go to Calypso's island and tell her to set Odysseus free. Hermes goes to find Calypso on her island. Calypso receives him warmly but flies into a rage when he tells her to release Odysseus. Nevertheless, Calypso tells Odysseus she has decided to let him go home. Odysseus assumes this is a trick and demands that Calypso swear a sacred oath that she is not plotting against him. She does, and then feeds and pampers him and tries to convince him to stay of his own free will. It doesn't work and he sails away on a raft. He sails for 18 days before Poseidon sees him, becomes angry, and summons a storm to thwart Odysseus. He is about to die but is saved by water goddess Ino, who gives him a magical scarf to protect him. He makes it to shore and falls asleep.

Book 6: Athena travels to a city near where Odysseus has landed and finds the Princess Nausicaa. Athena disguises herself as one of Nausicaa's friends and in a dream urges the princess to take a journey to the shore in order to wash her clothes. The next day, the princess and her maids travel to the beach and wake Odysseus, who stumbles naked into their midst. He talks to Nausicaa and she offers him clothing and hospitality in town. While he is bathing and dressing, Athena enchants him so that he seems even larger and more handsome than he is. Nausicaa tells him he cannot come to the palace with her because people will gossip, but if he comes independently and wins over her mother, he will be very welcome there.

Book 7: Athena disguises herself as a small child and puts herself in Odysseus' path. He asks her to guide him to the palace. She does and there he throws himself on the mercy of the queen and is seated at the king's high table as an honored guest. After dinner, the queen recognizes Odysseus's wearing as being those she'd made herself and questions where he got them. Odysseus tells her of being shipwrecked on Calypso's island and being trapped there seven years, of his raft trip and the storm and being rescued by the princess. King Alcinous promises to send him home the next day.

Book 8: Alcinous introduces Odysseus to his people and brings in the blind bard Demodocus to sing for him. The song is so beautiful that Odysseus cries. Then there are wrestling contests and they ask Odysseus to participate. Odysseus declines, but when he is taunted, he becomes angry and eventually challenges anyone who will listen to a sporting contest. To stop his boasting, the queen calls back the bard to sing some more. The feast continues and everyone gives Odysseus presents. He then convinces the bard to sing about the story of the Trojan Horse, but hearing the story makes him start crying again. Alcinous notices and asks Odysseus to recount his story.

Book 9: Odysseus tells the story of his journey from Troy. He and his men sacked Ismarus but were outnumbered and had to row away. They end up in the land of the lotus eaters, where people have forgotten their purpose, and they have to leave before anyone eats a lotus. Then they come to the island of the cyclops, Polyphemus. They break into his cave and eat all his cheese, not knowing that a giant lives there. When Polyphemus returns he traps them in the cave and eats two of Odysseus' men. The next day Odysseus and his men blind the Cyclops and then escape with his herd of sheep. Polyphemus asks Poseidon to curse Odysseus.

Book 10: Odysseus' ship stops at the home of Aeolus, master of the four winds, and he gives Odysseus a bag of winds to help blow his ship home. The ship's men break open the bag, assuming it contains gold, and end up blowing the ship back to Aeolus' island. Aeolus decides this means Odysseus is cursed and orders them to leave. Next they encounter the cannibalistic Laestrygonians and have to run away again. Next they get to the island of Circe, a sorceress, who turns some of Odysseus' crew into pigs. Odysseus goes to confront her, but Hermes stops him and gives him a magic herb to protect him. When he proves impervious to her magic, Circe correctly guesses who he is and offers him perfect hospitality. She changes his men back into humans at his request, and he and his comrades stay there for a year. Eventually, they depart for the House of Death.

Thought Questions (students consider while they read)

1. When Calypso is told she has to let Odysseus go, she does. Do you think she's just doing this because Zeus told her to, or because she wants to make

Odysseus happy even if it means he must leave?
2. Odysseus makes a calculated decision about how to win Nausicaa over. Do you think Odysseus' wiliness and cleverness is a positive or negative trait? Does it prevent him from being genuine with others?
3. The *Odyssey* is a sequel of sorts to the *Iliad*. There are many characters whose fates you learn about, but you are less invested in them if you haven't read the *Iliad*. Do you think this renders those portions less effective?
4. Would it be possible to tell the story of the Odyssey outside of the context of the Greek gods?
5. Why do you think Odysseus doesn't stay and investigate the Lotus Eaters?

Vocabulary (in order of appearance)

Book 5:

- supple: flexible, yielding
- bulwark: a fortification, a wall built for defense
- Pleiades: a constellation named for Atlas' seven daughters, who according to legend were placed in the sky by Zeus
- swell: a sea wave that never breaks

Book 6:

- lustrous: shiny, with luster
- soiled: dirty
- suppliant: a person pleading for something from someone else

Book 7:

- exile: one who has been banished from his homeland
- immortal: living forever
- luxuriant: lush, verdant
- succulent: tender or juicy

Book 8:

- rapturous: with great joy
- herald: a ceremonial official who makes announcements

Additional Homework

1. Odysseus takes part in a series of athletic events while in Phaeacia. Research the history of sports in ancient Greece and their importance to the world at the time. Are sports one of the most lasting legacies of ancient Greek culture? Write a paragraph defending your position.

Day 2 - Discussion of Thought Questions

1. When Calypso is told she has to let Odysseus go, she does. Do you think she's just doing this because Zeus told her to, or because she wants to make Odysseus happy even if it means he must leave?

   Time: 5-7 minutes

   Discussion: Odysseus tells Calypso how unhappy he is and she helps him prepare his raft and make sure he has provisions. But on the other hand, she's been ordered by much more powerful gods to do so. Odysseus clearly doesn't trust her--he asks for a solemn vow that she is not plotting against him--but since he doesn't trust anybody, that's not much of an indicator. She makes a play for his affections and he admits that she's much more beautiful than his wife, but when he makes it clear that he won't be happy unless he's returned to Ithaca, Calypso accepts his desires.

2. Odysseus makes a calculated decision about how to win Nausicaa over. Do you think Odysseus' wiliness and cleverness is a positive or negative trait? Does it prevent him from being genuine with others?

   Time: 10 minutes

   Discussion: There are multiple instances where Odysseus' cleverness saves the day — for instance, the Trojan Horse or the escape from Polyphemus' cave. But on the other hand, it's made clear that he trusts no-one (later in the book he plays a trick on his aged father for no discernible reason and refuses to admit his own identity). This probably distances him from others and makes it difficult for him to have genuine relationships. Perhaps this trait makes him a good hero but a difficult individual.

3. The *Odyssey* is a sequel of sorts to the *Iliad*. There are many characters whose fates you learn about, but you are less invested in them if you haven't read the *Iliad*. Do you think this renders those portions less effective?

Time: 7-10 minutes

Discussion: Students unfamiliar with the *Iliad* still have to hear about the fates of Ajax and Agamemnon. This may be a useful way to introduce the story of the *Iliad* to students who haven't read it, provide them with some background and perhaps convince them to do some additional reading. Talk about the stories and myths of a culture and how they provide background for the art it creates--are there stories everyone in the class would know merely by fleeting reference?

4. Would it be possible to tell the story of the Odyssey outside of the context of the Greek gods?

   Time: 5 minutes

   Discussion: Would the story be as effective without the notion of actual, motivated actors behind so many seemingly random coincidences in the story? What if Odysseus wasn't cursed and was just unlucky? The addition of the gods gives the story a more epic flavor--this must be important if super-beings are involved! On the other hand, the gods are so capricious that they function almost like coincidence in storytelling terms.

5. Why do you think Odysseus doesn't stay and investigate the Lotus Eaters?

   Time: 5 minutes

   Discussion: The lotus makes them forget that they want to get home, which is Odysseus' whole motivation throughout the story. The lotus eaters serve as his opposite, in fact, reminding him of what's important in their total neglect of it.

Day 2 - Short Answer Quiz

1. What does Poseidon do when he sees Odysseus afloat on his raft?

____

2. How does Ino save Odysseus from the storm at sea?

____

3. What is Odysseus' last-ditch attempt to save himself from drowning?

____

4. What does Nausicaa instruct Odysseus to do once he gets to her father's palace?

____

5. Why won't Athena appear undisguised to Odysseus?

____

6. Why is Queen Arete suspicious of Odysseus?

____

7. What is notable about Demodocus the bard?

___

8. What does Odysseus sharpen into an instrument to stab the Cyclops?

___

9. Who is Elpenor?

___

10. What does Hermes give Odysseus to protect him from Circe's spells?

___

Short Answer Quiz Key

1. Poseidon summons a storm to drown Odysseus.
2. She gives him a magic scarf to tie around his waist.
3. He prays to the river god, who calms the waves.
4. Win over the queen and "grasp her knees."
5. She is afraid of the wrath of Poseidon.
6. He is wearing clothes that she and her maids sewed.
7. He is blind.
8. Polyphemus' club.
9. A young sailor with Odysseus who falls off a roof on Circe's island and dies the day Odysseus and his men leave.
10. A magic herb called moly.

Day 2 - Crossword Puzzle

ACROSS

3. What are Nausicaa and her friends playing with when they find Odysseus?
4. Eating this makes you forget your purpose in life
5. Greek goddess of love
7. Odysseus' home
9. A minor goddess, often tied to nature somehow
13. Mythical one-eyed giant
15. What kind of wooden animal did the Greeks hide inside?
17. The bard in Alcinous' court
18. A circular object thrown as part of an athletic contest
19. Demodocus and Homer are both _____
20. A small harp-like instrument

DOWN

1. Metal cooking pot, often stirred over a fire
2. A human who eats other humans
6. A one-eyed giant
8. Who is Nausicaa's father?
10. Which god is angry at Odysseus?
11. What does Circe turn Odysseus' men into?
12. What kind of structure does Polyphemus live in?
14. Which wind do Odysseus' men set free?
16. To scoop, dig or poke out

Crossword Puzzle Answer Key

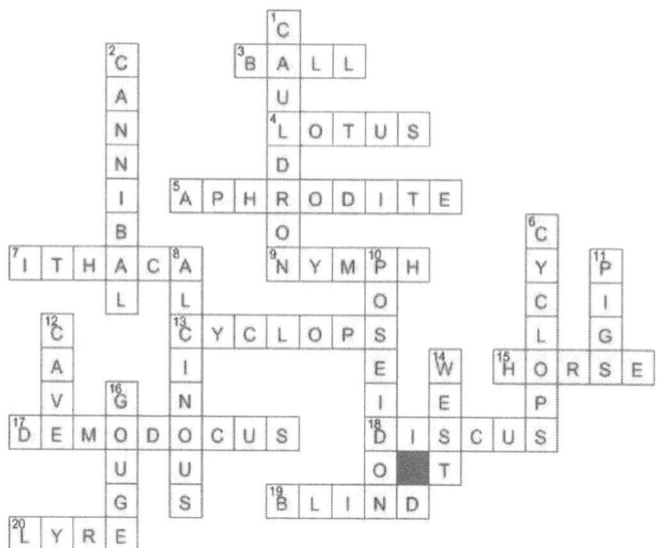

ACROSS

3. What are Nausicaa and her friends playing with when they find Odysseus?
4. Eating this makes you forget your purpose in life
5. Greek goddess of love
7. Odysseus' home
9. A minor goddess, often tied to nature somehow
13. Mythical one-eyed giant
15. What kind of wooden animal did the Greeks hide inside?
17. The bard in Alcinous' court
18. A circular object thrown as part of an athletic contest
19. Demodocus and Homer are both ____
20. A small harp-like instrument

DOWN

1. Metal cooking pot, often stirred over a fire
2. A human who eats other humans
6. A one-eyed giant
8. Who is Nausicaa's father?
10. Which god is angry at Odysseus?
11. What does Circe turn Odysseus' men into?
12. What kind of structure does Polyphemus live in?
14. Which wind do Odysseus' men set free?
16. To scoop, dig or poke out

Day 2 - Vocabulary Quiz

Terms	Answers
1. ____ supple	A. a person pleading for something from someone else
2. ____ bulwark	B. shiny, with luster
3. ____ Pleiades	C. a constellation named for Atlas' seven daughters, who according to legend were placed in the sky by Zeus
4. ____ swell	D. flexible, yielding
5. ____ lustrous	E. with great joy
6. ____ soiled	F. one who has been banished from his homeland
7. ____ suppliant	G. a fortification, a wall built for defense
8. ____ exile	H. dirty
9. ____ immortal	I. a ceremonial official who makes announcements
10. ____ luxuriant	J. lush, verdant
11. ____ succulent	K. living forever
12. ____ rapturous	L. tender or juicy
13. ____ herald	M. a sea wave that never breaks

Vocabulary Quiz Answer Key

1. D
2. G
3. C
4. M
5. B
6. H
7. A
8. F
9. K
10. J
11. L
12. E
13. I

Day 2 - Classroom Activities

1. Who are These Gods, Anyway?

   Kind of Activity: Research
   Objective: Students will understand more about the background of several major characters in the *Odyssey*
   Common Core State Standards: CCSS.ELA-Literacy.CCRA.R.3 ; CCSS.ELA-Literacy.CCRA.SL.4
   Time: 45 minutes (with the bulk assigned as homework)

   Structure:

   Separate the students into groups. Each group should choose a deity featured heavily in the text—for example Athena, Zeus or Hermes—and research that god's character and duties in terms of Greek mythology. They should find out about their role in the *Iliad* and various other myths, and be able to explain how their assigned god fits into the pantheon.

   They can talk about the evolution of their chosen deity's personality and set of powers over time, and discuss the ways that this particular god might represent what was important to Ancient Greek culture at large. Each group should present an oral report designed to spark class discussion. In the discussion, talk about how this background knowledge informs their understanding of the story of the *Odyssey*.

   Ideans for Differentiated Instruction:

   -Students could work individually on this project rather than in groups.

   -The presentations could be expanded into longer, written reports researched and produced over several days.

   -Reports could include audio or visual aspects designed to illustrate the evolution of representations of the specific deity over time.

   Assessment Ideas:
   -Evaluate student notes and presentations, having students turn in their research, notes, and powerpoint slides or handouts.

2. Court of Gods

   Kind of Activity: Role Play

Objective: to emphasize the importance of point of view when telling any story
Common Core State Standards: CCSS.ELA-Literacy.CCRA.SL.3 ; CCSS.ELA-Literacy.CCRA.SL.1
Time: 25 minutes

Structure:

As a class, discuss Poseidon's argument that Odysseus deserves to be punished, and Odysseus' argument that he should be allowed to make his way home. Analyze the two positions as they relate to ancient and modern conceptions of morality, responsibility, vengeance and retribution. Ask students to talk about the conception of "justice" in the *Odyssey* in general and how it relates to the society in which the poem was created. Talk about modern texts that also deal with the concept of justice; how has the concept changed over time and with cultural shifts?

Next, assign students the roles of various characters in the *Odyssey* and have them debate the question in their roles. A section of the class designated as a jury can then vote to determine who has made the better case and what a fairer course of action would be for all concerned.

Ideans for Differentiated Instruction:

-Your most outgoing students, perhaps those with acting experience, will probably be most comfortable in the acting roles.

-This activity could take place over a few days so students have more time to prepare original and individual arguments.

Assessment Ideas:

-Evaluate how well individual students can accurately recount events of the novel and display an understanding of the importance of framing when it comes to making persuasive arguments.

-Have students write up their arguments as briefing memos, which should be turned in to the instructor for evaluation.

Day 3 - Reading Assignment

Books 11-14

Common Core Objectives

- CCSS.ELA-Literacy.CCRA.R.6 Assess how point of view or purpose shapes the content and style of a text.
- CCSS.ELA-Literacy.CCRA.R.3 Analyze how and why individuals, events, or ideas develop and interact over the course of a text.
- CCSS.ELA-Literacy.CCRA.SL.2 Integrate and evaluate information presented in diverse media and formats, including visually, quantitatively, and orally.
- CCSS.ELA-Literacy.CCRA.R.9 Analyze how two or more texts address similar themes or topics in order to build knowledge or to compare the approaches the authors take.

Note that it is perfectly fine to expand any day's work into two days depending on the characteristics of the class, particularly if the class will engage in all of the suggested classroom exercises and activities and discuss all of the thought questions.

Content Summary for Teachers

Book 11: Odysseus continues to tell his story before the court of Alcinous. In it, Odysseus performs a ritual to summon ghosts and get to the Underworld. Odysseus finds the ghost of Elpinor, who asks to be buried properly, and the prophet Tiresias, who says that as long as his men don't eat the Cattle of the Sun, everyone can get home alive. But if they do eat the Cattle of the Sun, only Odysseus will get home, and only after much hardship. Odysseus also encounters his mother, who says she died of grief because he never came home. He continues speaking to a crowd of female ghosts, all famous women, until present-day is interrupted in his story by Queen Arete, who praises him and promises gifts. He continues his story, in which he encounters the ghost of Agamemnon, who describes his own death and warns Odysseus not to trust his wife. Odysseus also sees Achilles, Ajax, Tantalus, Sisyphus and Heracles, and hopes to see more but has to flee when a horde of ghosts attack.

Book 12: Odysseus and his men return to Circe's island and give Elpenor the burial he asked for. Circe tells him about the Sirens and advises him on how to resist them, as well as how to survive Scylla and Charybdis. She then reminds him not to let his men eat the Cattle of the Sun. They set out, encounter and survive the Sirens, and get past Scylla and Charybdis. They get to the island of the Sun, and Odysseus warns his men not to eat the cattle. But then they get stranded there by unfavorable winds for a month, the men are starving, and Eurylochus encourages them to feast on the cattle rather than die. They do, and though Odysseus scolds them when he finds out, they set sail again. Their ship is immediately hit by a storm that kills everyone but

Odysseus, and sends our hero out on a raft. He drifts for nine days until he gets to Calypso's island.

Book 13: Odysseus sets sail for Ithaca in a new ship given to him by King Alcinous. Poseidon, still angry at Odysseus, wrecks the ship as it gets back to its home port. Meanwhile, Odysseus wakes up and doesn't recognize his homeland. He curses the Phaeacians for leaving him there. He wants to explore and determine where he is, but that would mean leaving his treasure open to bandits. Athena shows up disguised as a shepherd and tells him he is in Ithaca. He is overjoyed, but decides to lie and pretend he's never been to Ithaca before; he claims to be a former soldier who killed a man and had to become a fugitive. Athena changes her form to that of a woman and praises Odysseus for his guile. She tells him Penelope is still waiting for him; together they bury his treasures so that thieves won't take them. Athena then transforms Odysseus into an old man in order to fool Penelope and her suitors, and leaves for Sparta to fetch Telemachus home.

Book 14: Odysseus, disguised, goes to the house of an old swineherd who is still loyal to his missing master. The swineherd takes the "stranger" in and talks of how he misses Odysseus. He also complains about the gluttony of Penelope's suitors. Odysseus tells the swineherd that Odysseus will return soon, but the swineherd assures him that his master must be dead. Odysseus then tells him an elaborately fabricated life-story, which includes an encounter with Odysseus (who he maintains is on his way home) and a narrow escape from enslavement. The swineherd accuses Odysseus of lying, which he is, and Odysseus laments the man's "dark, suspicious heart."

Thought Questions (students consider while they read)

1. Agamemnon warns Odysseus not to trust women. Why do you think this is?
2. Alcinous decides that all his nobles must give treasure to Odysseus and says they should tax their subjects to pay for it. Do you think this is a fair way to govern?
3. The Phaeacians see their ship wrecked, presumably by Poseidon, and their first response is not to rail against the god but to sacrifice many bulls to him. What does this say about the relation of the ancient Greeks to their gods?
4. Why do you think the swineherd loved Odysseus so much?
5. Why do you think the story of Agamemnon's murder is repeated so many times in the *Odyssey*?

Vocabulary (in order of appearance)

Book 11:

- pyre: a mound of flammable material, often used for burning dead bodies in a funeral rite
- shambling: shuffling, with a halting gait
- flitter: to move quickly but without purpose
- magnanimous: generous, kind
- ebb: decline, diminish

Book 12:

- grisly: horrible, disgusting
- scourge: a menace
- strait: a channel of water connecting two large bodies of water or seas

Book 13:

- blunder: wander clumsily
- keel: the timber underlying the structure of a ship

Book 14:

- stockade: a fence made of stakes
- paltry: scant, insufficient

Additional Homework

1. Odysseus speaks to many ghosts in the House of the Dead. Pick one and research his or her backstory, trying to figure out what he or she would have to disclose as a ghost.

Made in the USA
San Bernardino, CA
21 February 2015